UNBREAKABLE

Unbreakable

Unlock a Life of True Freedom and Purpose in an Upside-Down World

Nick LeMonds, MDiv

©2025 All Rights Reserved. No portion of this book may be reproduced, stored in a retrieval system, or transmitted in any form or by any means—electronic, mechanical, photocopy, recording, scanning, or other—except for brief quotations in critical reviews or articles without the prior permission of the author.

Published by Game Changer Publishing

Paperback ISBN: 978-1-966659-15-0

Hardcover ISBN: 978-1-966659-16-7

Digital ISBN: 978-1-966659-17-4

www.GameChangerPublishing.com

DEDICATION

For Yolanda, whose love has been my anchor; for Aliza and Raquel, whose joy lights my way; and for our unborn son, a beacon of hope.

To my mentors and friends who've shaped me with their wisdom and encouragement.

And to all who long for deeper freedom and purpose— may this work be a companion on your journey.

READ THIS FIRST

Thank you for embarking on this journey toward unbreakable freedom and purpose! As my way of saying thanks, I've prepared exclusive bonuses and a no-charge coaching call—no strings attached! Simply scan the QR code to claim your gifts and explore how we can clarify your vision, ignite your transformation, and discuss whether working together is the next step for you.

Scan the QR Code Here:

UNBREAKABLE

UNLOCK A LIFE OF TRUE FREEDOM AND
PURPOSE IN AN UPSIDE-DOWN WORLD

NICK LEMONDS, MDIV

FOREWORD

The gathering had begun, and I remember standing in the back of the room and noticing a well-dressed young man who slipped in quietly. Although he did not want to stand out, he was wearing a black suit with a tie, careful not to be underdressed at the unfamiliar meeting. The young man in the suit was Nick LeMonds. Little did I know that day would mark the beginning of an authentic friendship—one that would shape my life and touch the lives of many who came to know Nick.

In hindsight, I am sure Nick felt a bit odd showing up to a new place, not knowing what to wear or anyone there, but I would soon learn to appreciate Nick's courage to face new situations as one of the things I love most about him. As I have had a front-row seat to so much of the story you are about to read, I sense it is important for you, the reader, to know just how true to life the story is in the following pages.

Perhaps you have heard the phrase, "Don't meet your heroes." The people you look up to sometimes can disappoint you the most. Sometimes the letdown is because of unrealistic expectations. At other times, the audio just does not match the video,

FOREWORD

what is taught is not what is lived. This was not my experience with Nick. Nick's words and life are authentic and in sync.

As one who has walked beside Nick in friendship for well over a decade, his authentic desire for life transformation is both personally embodied and passionately coached in the lives of others. Nick connects genuinely with people, so be prepared to connect with Nick's story and find a companion in this book.

The book you are about to read is a real story of transformation. Nick writes as a companion as he shares his moving testimony through the various moments and stages of growth and integrated wholeness. You may soon discover that the book is not only about Nick's story, but it is also about your story as well.

At the end of each chapter are insightful questions and practices that are invaluable tools for you to journey toward greater transformation and change within your own life. The book is written in a conversational and encouraging style, offering motivating stories along with empowering steps for your own transformational journey ahead. I hope this short foreword encourages you to begin the first chapter right now—because the best is yet to come!

Art Matheny, DMIn
Lead pastor Living Vine Church
Spiritual Director

CONTENTS

Introduction	xiii
1. Shattered Illusions *Breaking the Chains of the Past*	1
2. The Ache of Misalignment *Finding Integrity and Wholeness*	17
3. The Call to Courage *Facing Fear and Finding Your True Path*	35
4. The Power of Purpose *Fueling a Life of Meaning and Impact*	52
5. From Setbacks to Stepping Stones *Building Resilience Through Adversity*	70
6. From Self to Service *Discovering Fulfillment in Giving*	85
7. Living in Harmony *Integrating Body, Soul, and Spirit*	99
8. Rooted in Faith *Building a Life That Stands Strong*	114
9. The Strength in Softness *Embracing Vulnerability as Power*	131
10. The Unfinished Journey *Embracing the Path of Ongoing Transformation*	145
11. A Manifesto for an Unbreakable Life	160
Conclusion	171
Bibliography	175
Thank You for Reading my Book!	181

INTRODUCTION
WAKING UP TO A NEW LIFE

Awakening. It's the moment the fog lifts, the veil drops, and the truth emerges. It's the wake-up call, the breaking of the dawn after a long, dark night. For too long, we drift through life on autopilot, living in a trance of inauthenticity. My name is Nick LeMonds, and I've emerged from that trance, stepping into the light with a fierce determination and a singular purpose: to help others find their way, to illuminate the path forward in this disorienting, upside-down world.

In a society that feels increasingly chaotic and disconnected, I offer my story as a beacon, a guidepost for those who feel lost in their own struggles, doubts, and fears. I grew up in a small town in Oregon, where I fell early into the traps of addiction—drugs, alcohol, women—all of which led me to places of deep despair and bondage. But I've emerged on the other side, not just surviving but thriving, thanks to an unwavering commitment to personal growth, spiritual encounters, and the relentless pursuit of authenticity.

This book is a lifeline. It's for those who feel trapped by their circumstances, who are haunted by the specters of their past and

INTRODUCTION

uncertain about their future. My message is simple but profound: Transformation is not only possible—it's required. It is our mandate, our calling, our duty while we are here on this earth to continually evolve, to transcend the limitations of our past, and to step boldly into the fullness of who we are meant to be.

I wrote this book for those who crave something deeper. For those who are tired of surface-level living and want to tap into the wellspring of purpose, meaning, and true fulfillment. I wrote it to infuse love and courage into your soul. It's intended to be more than just a good read but to become a catalyst for real change, a tool that will show up in your everyday life. Because I've been there. I know what it's like to live under the crushing weight of failure, to chase hollow dreams, to buy into destructive lies. But I also know what it's like to break free, find the way out, and live a life marked by passion, purpose, and divine guidance.

This book is not just inspirational; it's practical. It's filled with invitations—questions, and challenges designed to help you break free from the chains of your past, align your life with your deepest values, and step into your God-given divine purpose. It's about transformation on a cellular level, not just of your mind but of your heart, your spirit, and your entire being.

FINDING YOUR WAY OUT

I want you to know that change is not about gaining more knowledge. Tim Grover, one of the most respected coaches in the world, said it best: "The only thing that transforms potential into success is relentless, applied effort." This is not about amassing more information or waiting for that one "aha" moment that will magically change everything, although this book will have some of those, too. True transformation doesn't happen until you take that knowledge, that understanding, and apply it, integrate it into all of your life until you *become* it. You execute on it not just for yourself but for the sake of those around you—for your family, your friends, your communities you are a part of, and even for the strangers who might be watching you more closely than you realize.

Transformation is about becoming someone new. It's about refusing to be molded by the systems, structures, and cultural norms that no longer serve you. Instead, it requires an ongoing renewal of your mind, a willingness to examine and challenge every thought, belief, and assumption. It's about shedding layers of guilt, shame, fear, and regret, stepping fully into a God-given identity rooted in truth and purpose. In doing so, you don't just live more authentically for yourself—you also become a source of light and hope for others, offering your gifts, your presence, and your love to help shape a more meaningful world. More on this later.

THE JOURNEY OF BECOMING

This book is for the brave ones, those who are willing to confront their pain, their past, and their patterns with an open heart and a willing spirit. It's not for those looking for a quick fix or an easy path. It's for those who are ready to do the deep work and who understand that real change requires both courage and humility. You see, I didn't just wake up one day transformed. My journey has been shaped by countless failures, by moments of despair, and by hitting rock bottom over and over again. But each time, I choose to rise. I choose to learn. I choose to keep going, fueled by a relentless desire to become the man I know I am meant to be.

And now, I want to share that journey with you. I want to offer you the same hope and guidance that I received, the same tools and strategies that helped me turn my life around. Because I believe that if I can do it, anyone can. The power of transformation is within reach for every single one of us. It's not reserved for the special, the privileged, or the lucky. It's available to anyone who is willing to do the work, to face their fears, to step into the unknown, and to trust that something greater is guiding them.

A CALL TO ACTION

This book is an invitation to stand up and take responsibility for your life. It's a call to step out of the shadows of complacency and into the light of possibility. It's a challenge to stop settling for less than what you are capable of and to start living a life that is fully alive, fully engaged, and fully aligned with your true purpose.

My hope is that this book will ignite a fire in your soul, that it will inspire you to live boldly and courageously, and that it will equip you with the tools you need to make a lasting impact in your world. Whether you're struggling with addiction, stuck in a toxic relationship, or simply feeling lost and directionless, this book is for you. It's for anyone who knows, deep down, that they are meant for more in this upside-down world and are called to make a massive difference around them.

Transformation is a journey, not a destination. It's a process that unfolds over time through every decision, every action, every step we take. And it's a journey that we're all on, whether we realize it or not. So, let this book be your guide. Let it be your companion on the road to becoming the person you were created to be. Let it help you find your way out of the darkness and into the light, where you can shine as brightly as you were always meant to.

Because, in the end, it's not just about transforming your own life. It's about being a light for others, about leaving a legacy of love, hope, and purpose that will continue to inspire and uplift long after you're gone. That's my prayer for you as you read these pages: that you will not only find your own path to freedom, but

INTRODUCTION

also become a beacon of light for others, showing them the way, and leading them home.

Welcome to your transformation. Welcome to a new way of living, a new way of being. It's time to wake up. It's time to live fully. It's time to become who you were always meant to be. It's time to live with a level of freedom and purpose you were created to live every single day of your life.

ONE
SHATTERED ILLUSIONS
BREAKING THE CHAINS OF THE PAST

*Then you will experience for yourselves the truth,
and the truth will free you.*

I woke up one day and stared into the mirror, but I couldn't recognize the person looking back. It wasn't just my reflection that felt alien; it was the sheer disgust, the overwhelming hatred I felt towards myself. I was only seven or eight years old, but the emotions were raw and visceral. That image of myself—worthless, disgusting, broken—was burned into my mind. From that day forward, everything changed. Something shifted inside me. It was as if a switch had flipped in my brain, and suddenly, the world around me felt heavy and suffocating. We'll dive deeper into this story, and what led me to such stark emotions later in the book (see Chapter 5), but for now, I want you to feel the weight of that morning–because it's where my journey to freedom and purpose really began.

Before that moment, I was just an ordinary kid. I loved playing sports, running around with friends, and being a part of my small community in Oregon. I did well in school, was popular, and had a life that seemed perfectly fine on the outside. But none of that mattered on the day I began to see myself differently. That sense of inadequacy, of being somehow wrong or defective, grew over the years. It was like an infection, spreading slowly but surely, contaminating my thoughts and emotions.

THE FIRST TASTE OF ESCAPE

It all came to a head on a sweltering summer night when I was 12 years old. It was the end of my fifth-grade year, and I was looking forward to starting junior high in the fall. I was on the brink of adolescence, teetering between childhood innocence and the complicated world of teenage years. That night, I was introduced to the most potent numbing agents on the planet—marijuana, alcohol, tobacco, and pornography—all in one go.

I didn't plan it. I didn't wake up that morning thinking, "Today is the day I start destroying my life." It just happened. The opportunity presented itself, and I was weak, unprepared, and ignorant of the consequences. I had no idea that those first experiences with these substances and images would set me on a path of self-destruction that would take over a decade to escape.

For the first time in my life, I felt powerful.

> *"Addiction begins with the hope that something 'out there' can instantly fill up the emptiness inside."*
> – Jeane Kilbourne

The substances numbed me and dulled the pain that had been gnawing at me for years. I felt invincible, free from the relentless self-hatred and shame that had become my constant companions. In those fleeting moments, I wasn't thinking about how I was a mistake or a defective human being. I was just... numb. And for a 12-year-old who had been drowning in negative thoughts, that feeling was intoxicating.

But it was all a lie. Those substances and images promised freedom but delivered bondage. They whispered sweet nothings about escape but wrapped me in chains of addiction and despair. What I thought would be a doorway to freedom became a prison, and I was locked in tighter than ever.

It took me years to understand that the chains I wore weren't forged from drugs or images alone—they were anchored in the stories I believed about myself. The patterns that kept me locked in self-destruction were guided by unseen scripts running through my mind. When a person begins to challenge these ingrained narratives, they start to see that genuine freedom is never found in external escapes. Real liberation emerges as we confront the inner voices that define who we are and who we can become.

DESCENT INTO DARKNESS

The next 12 years were a living nightmare. From that fateful night, until I was 24, I spiraled into the depths of addiction and destruction. By the time I was 15, I had been arrested half a dozen times. I had been in and out of drug rehab twice, and I was expelled from junior high and sentenced to finish my seventh and eighth grades at an alternative school.

That alternative school was a gathering place for outcasts like me—kids who were trying to escape their own pain, who used drugs and alcohol to numb the traumas they were experiencing in their own lives and didn't know how to face. It was there that I found a sense of belonging, but it was a toxic, destructive kind of acceptance. We were all running from something, and instead of finding a way out, we dug ourselves deeper into the pit.

> *"We are only as sick as our secrets."*
> – Sigmund Freud

By the time I was 17, I was a full-blown addict. Alcohol, drugs, women—anything to keep the pain and voices in my head at bay. I had been arrested a dozen more times and had stood before judges and lawyers who saw me as just another lost cause. I went through another round of rehab, but it didn't stick. Nothing did. The cycle of addiction and self-destruction was relentless.

Author Anne Lamott, known for her raw honesty about addiction and recovery, once wrote, "Hope begins in the dark, the stubborn hope that if you just show up and try to do the right thing, the dawn will come." But for me, the dawn felt perpetually out of reach. Each failed attempt at recovery only deepened my despair, convincing me that I was beyond saving. I was trapped in the shadows, unable to see a way out, even though a part of me desperately wanted to believe in the possibility of light.

At 18, I started dealing narcotics. It was a dangerous, chaotic life, but I didn't care. I was numb, indifferent. Over the next five years, I was arrested another 20 or 30 times, accumulating felony charges, court appearances, and a mountain of legal trouble. I was a wreck, spiraling further and further into darkness.

BREAKING POINT

There's a quote by Augustine that says, "You have made us for yourself, O Lord and our hearts are restless until they rest in you." My heart was restless and tortured, but I was looking for peace in all the wrong places. I thought drugs, alcohol, and women would fill the void, but they only made it deeper. I was living in a nightmare of my own making, trapped in a prison with no hope of escape.

One night, after yet another arrest, I found myself alone,

sitting on the cold concrete floor of a jail cell. I was 24, and my life was in shambles. As I sat there, I began to realize that all the things I had been chasing—freedom, power, escape—were illusions. They had shattered, leaving me with nothing but the painful truth that I was utterly lost. I had hit rock bottom, and for the first time in a long time, I felt something other than numbness. I felt desperate.

I later learned the words of Jesus: "The thief comes only to steal and kill and destroy; I have come that they may have life, and have it to the full". I had been robbed—of my youth, my innocence, my potential—by the thief of addiction. I didn't know it until later, but Jesus offered a different path, a way out of the darkness. I didn't know God or have much of an understanding of who He is, but I knew I needed help, and that night, desperate, I found it.

> "Every act of rebellion expresses a nostalgia for innocence and an appeal to the essence of being."
> – Albert Camus

Only later did I come to realize that true freedom doesn't hinge solely on distancing ourselves from harmful behaviors. It also involves recognizing that we were never meant to live trapped by old identities or imprisoned by false perceptions. The journey beyond the breaking point calls for a renewal of the mind —a willingness to see ourselves through a more truthful lens. This is the doorway that leads from darkness into the possibility of a new life defined by purpose and inner strength.

THE ROAD TO RECOVERY

Recovery didn't happen overnight; it was a long, painful journey of confronting the demons I'd been fleeing. Facing the shame, self-hatred, and pain that fueled my addiction required relentless commitment. One of the toughest steps was taking a moral inventory—listing those I'd hurt, the bridges I'd burned, the relationships I'd destroyed. Seeing the wreckage of my actions was both humbling and heartbreaking.

Among those I had wronged was Randy, a woman who had been a significant part of my life. We shared dreams, but my addiction overshadowed everything. Consumed by fear and selfishness, we made the painful decision to have an abortion. She wanted to build a life together, but I abandoned her when she needed me most.

In an attempt to make amends, I reached out to Randy. I offered a sincere apology, owning my mistakes without excuses. But she wasn't ready to forgive; her wounds were still too deep. This painful encounter taught me that making amends isn't about seeking forgiveness but about taking responsibility, regardless of the outcome.

These early steps exposed raw emotions but also paved the way for genuine healing. I learned that recovery wasn't just about abstaining from substances; it was about transforming who I was and how I related to the world. Some forgave me—others did not. Each interaction taught me valuable lessons about empathy, patience, and the complexities of healing.

In facing these hard truths, I discovered that real healing involves more than regret or surface-level change. It requires reshaping the very beliefs that fuel our actions. Each step of recovery, from acknowledging our failures to taking responsibility for the harm we've caused, offers a chance to release old ways of thinking. As we learn to recognize and dismantle the limiting beliefs that once ruled our lives, we create space for something new—an identity no longer defined by past mistakes.

This journey taught me that true transformation is profoundly internal, requiring a renewed mind and spirit to embrace the freedom of a new life.

Tim Grover, a renowned trainer of elite athletes, once said, "You can't change what's going on around you until you start changing what's going on within you." That's what recovery was for me—an inside job. It was about changing my mindset, my beliefs, and my relationship with myself and the world. It was about breaking free from the chains of my past and stepping into a new, authentic life.

FINDING PURPOSE IN PAIN

My journey wasn't just about getting clean. It was about discovering who I truly was beneath the layers of addiction and self-hatred. I realized that my pain, my struggles, and my mistakes weren't just random events—they were shaping and refining me. I began to see my life through a different lens, not as a series of failures but as a story of redemption.

I found strength as I continued on in the words of Paul, who wrote, "We also glory in our sufferings, because we know that suffering produces perseverance; perseverance, character; and character, hope." Looking back now, I could see the suffering I was experiencing was actually working *for* me and was producing a strength and resilience I never knew I had within me. It had forged a character in me that was unbreakable, and with that character came hope. Hope that my story could help others. Hope that my life could be more than the sum of my mistakes. Hope that I could make a difference, not just for myself, but for anyone who felt trapped by their own chains of addiction and despair.

Over time, I learned that the fires of suffering don't merely burn us—they refine us. Just as intense heat purifies metal, life's hardest moments can strip away the falsehoods and illusions, revealing a more resilient core beneath. Recognizing this truth empowers us. Instead of seeing pain as pointless or limiting, we can view it as preparation for the unique assignment that awaits each of us. Through these trials, we are shaped into the people we were always meant to be, capable of living with greater clarity, compassion, and conviction.

EMBRACING YOUR JOURNEY TO FREEDOM

This chapter has explored the depths of my own struggles, not just to share my story but to illuminate your path as well. It's about understanding that every challenge and every pain point can lead to profound personal growth and freedom. Now, as we move toward concluding this chapter, I invite you to pause and reflect deeply on your own experiences.

> *"What lies behind us and what lies before us are tiny matters compared to what lies within us."*
> – Ralph Waldo Emerson

At the end of each chapter of this book, you'll find a dedicated space to delve deep into your inner world—a place where you can actively engage with the stories, beliefs, and patterns that shape your life. Through powerful questions, insightful reflections, and practical exercises, these sections are crafted to guide you on your journey toward true freedom and purpose in the 21st century in which we live. Use these tools to challenge your perspectives, transform your experiences, and empower yourself to make meaningful, lasting changes. Embrace this opportunity to become unbreakable in an upside-down world.

As you prepare to look inward, consider that genuine transformation doesn't arise from chance. It unfolds when we dare to examine our own hearts, beliefs, and motives. By becoming aware of the internal dialogue that drives our choices, we begin to understand that the path to freedom doesn't lie in rearranging outer circumstances, but in reorienting how we see ourselves. The reflections and exercises you are about to engage in will help you discern these hidden patterns and empower you to chart a new course forward.

YOUR UNBREAKABLE JOURNEY

1. Invitation to Reflection

> Find a quiet, comfortable space where you won't be disturbed. Close your eyes for a moment and take a few deep breaths. Allow yourself to settle into a place of peace and openness. This is your time to explore your inner world with honesty and compassion.

2. Metaphorical Imagery

> Imagine standing in front of a grand mirror that reflects not just your outward appearance but the depths of your soul. Some parts are clear and luminous, while others are fogged and distorted by the illusions you've held onto. Today, you're going to begin wiping away the fog to see your true self more clearly.

3. Guided Self-Inquiry

> **Recall a time you felt "less than" or unworthy. If you had to name the thought or belief behind that feeling, what might it be—even if you're only guessing?**

Think back to a specific moment—maybe you hesitated to speak up in a group, or felt overshadowed by someone else's achievements. Imagine the inner voice behind that hesitation. Even if you're unsure, give it a name (like "I don't deserve success" or "I'm not smart enough") so you can begin to see it more clearly.

Which memories or experiences might have planted or reinforced that belief?

Pinpoint an event, a conversation, or even a pattern (big or small) that caused you to internalize that negative message. Was it a critical remark from someone you respected, or a repeated incident where you felt overlooked? Recognizing where that belief "took root" helps you trace its influence through your life story.

How has this perspective on your worth influenced your decisions, relationships, or growth up to now?

Reflect on the ripple effect: Has it kept you silent in key moments, led you to sabotage opportunities, or made you overcompensate in certain areas? Noticing these impacts can be a wake-up call, showing just how powerful these hidden beliefs can be—and why challenging them is so essential.

We all have crippling self-talk at times, and at some level, that violates the *truth* about our experience down here on earth. These questions are really a chance to become curious and aware of internal conversations that are happening. When we become curious, we are open now to begin exploring beliefs that are no longer serving us. In that place, we are able to shift or transform those conversations to more powerful conversations that empower us. You cannot shift what you cannot see. Take your time to write down your thoughts, allowing whatever arises to flow freely onto the page.

_____
_____
_____
_____
_____

4. Compassionate Engagement

As you reflect, treat yourself with the utmost kindness. Acknowledge that these beliefs were often formed as protective mechanisms in response to past pain or trauma. Recognize the courage it takes to face them now. Also know that these beliefs that were formed ultimately led you to "win" in life. They helped you get what you want at some level. Our goal is to identify them, dissect them, and decide if they are no longer serving you anymore. If they are not serving, it's time to uproot them. Be patient, this is an ongoing journey.

5. Deepening Awareness Exercise

Letter to Your Younger Self

Step 1: Visualize yourself at the age when you first began to feel these limiting beliefs. In my case, as described in this chapter, it'd be at around the age of seven or eight.

Step 2: Write a letter to this younger version of yourself. Offer the understanding, support, and love that you needed then.
What words of comfort would you share?
What truths would you want your younger self to know?

Step 3: Read the letter aloud to yourself, embracing the emotions that surface.

6. Reframing Challenges

Identify one predominant limiting belief you've discovered.

Original Belief: Write it down as it currently exists in your mind.

Example: "I am unworthy of love because of my past mistakes."

_____
_____
_____
_____
_____

Now, reframe this belief into an empowering truth.

Empowering Truth: Transform it into a positive declaration.

Example: "I am worthy of love and forgiveness, and my past does not define my future."

_____
_____
_____
_____
_____

7. Incorporating Wisdom

Reflect on the words of psychologist Carl Rogers:
"The curious paradox is that when I accept myself just as I am, then I can change."

Consider how accepting yourself—with all your imperfections and past experiences—can be the catalyst for true transformational change.

8. Actionable Steps

Commit to one tangible action this week that aligns with embracing your true self and releasing illusions. Assign a "by-when" to it if it's applicable. When you put yourself at stake for a specific time you commit to the action, the percentage of actually following through goes through the roof.

Possible Actions:

Begin a daily mindfulness or meditation practice to stay connected with your inner truth.

Share your reflections with a trusted friend or support group to build connections. (By-when will I share this? What day? What time? With whom?)

Your Chosen Action: Write down the specific step you will take.

_____
_____
_____
_____

9. Personal Commitment

Craft a personal declaration or commitment to solidify your intention moving forward. The goal is to begin. Your commitments will shift and adapt over time, but the goal is to get started.

Example: "I commit to honoring my authentic self and releasing the false beliefs that no longer serve me. I embrace my journey toward freedom with courage and hope."

Your Commitment Statement: Write your own declaration statement here.

_____
_____
_____
_____
_____

10. Vision of Empowerment

Close your eyes and envision a future where you are free from these chains. See yourself living authentically, embracing each day with confidence and joy. Feel the lightness in your spirit as you move forward, unencumbered by past illusions.

Hold onto this vision. Let it inspire you as you continue your journey toward true liberation.

Reflection:
Take a few moments to reflect on what you've written. How does it feel to confront these illusions? What emotions come up? Be gentle with yourself. This is hard work, but it's the kind of work that leads to true transformation.

FINAL ENCOURAGEMENT

You have taken a brave and significant step. Confronting and dismantling long-held illusions isn't easy, but it's a profound act of self-love and empowerment. This is also not a "one-off." These powerful illusions have a way of coming back even after dismantling. In that space, you get to choose to confront and dismantle it again, and again, and again, and again—and that is okay. Remember the words of author and activist James Baldwin:

"Not everything that is faced can be changed, but nothing can be changed until it is faced."

Continue to face each day with the knowledge that you are capable of incredible transformation. Your past does not dictate your future, and every moment is an opportunity to step into the fullness of who you are meant to be.

EMBRACE YOUR JOURNEY

This is not just an exercise—it's the beginning of a new chapter in your life. Revisit these reflections whenever you feel the shadows of illusion creeping back. Each time you do, you'll strengthen your resolve and move closer to the freedom and fulfillment you deserve.

Remember, you are not alone. Each step you take lights the way for others to follow.

Your journey towards freedom and purpose starts now.

TWO
THE ACHE OF MISALIGNMENT
FINDING INTEGRITY AND WHOLENESS

The integrity of the honest keeps them on track;
the deviousness of crooks brings them to ruin.

It was a familiar feeling—being on the run, looking over my shoulder, ducking into alleyways to avoid the glaring lights of police cars. The warrants were out for my arrest because I had absconded from a drug court program that was supposed to save my life. Drug court was no joke. I had to see a judge weekly, attend multiple classes, and submit to urine analysis tests several times a week. It was a relentless routine that kept me accountable, but at that time, I was not ready for accountability. I was not ready to be clean. I wasn't ready to be sober.

The thrill of selling narcotics was my escape, my version of "living." The chaos, the adrenaline—it was intoxicating in its own right. Money flowed easily. There were endless parties, hotels, bars, girls, and a parade of so-called friends at every turn. It was a lifestyle that made me feel invincible, but that invincibility was a lie—a powerful and seductive illusion. I thought I had control, but in reality, I was spiraling further and further out of it.

Illusions can only sustain you for so long before reality comes crashing in. That crash happened when I found myself completely out of money. My phone was cut off, the drugs were gone, and I was in a fog of withdrawal. I had loaned out all my products, expecting those friends to come through with payment, but not a single one showed up. I was left with nothing—no drugs, no cash, not even a pack of cigarettes or a drop of alcohol. The silence of my phone was deafening, and with every passing hour, the walls of my illusion crumbled.

WHEN THE MASK FALLS OFF

Desperation led me to venture out under the cover of night. With warrants hanging over my head, I had been careful to stay indoors, only going out when I had a guaranteed ride or when shielded by darkness. But now, I had no choice but to walk. I crept through town, darting between shadows, hiding in bushes when a car approached, and sprinting across the highway when the coast was clear. I made a loop around the town, visiting 12 different people—each one I considered a friend, each one a potential lifeline.

But door after door, I was met with excuses and empty promises. "I'll pay you back next week," "I don't have it right now, but I can get some for you soon," and even "Can you get me high?" The nerve of it! They had the audacity to ask me for more when I had nothing left. It was infuriating. Each encounter drove home the truth that had been there all along: these weren't real friends. They were just people looking for their next hit, their next escape, using me just as I had used them.

In that stark moment, I began to sense a truth I had long resisted: the patterns we cling to do more than just shape our actions; they define the quality of our existence. This was no mere inconvenience—this was a soul-deep ache born of living a life detached from who I truly was. When we live out of alignment with our core identity, every disappointment cuts deeper, every betrayal stings sharper, and every moment of silence amplifies the emptiness within. It's a slow erosion of the spirit, a weight pressing down on the heart until we hardly recognize ourselves beneath the burden.

LAST STOP AT MIKE'S HOUSE

The final stop was at my buddy Mike's house, my last hope to scrape together something to get back on my feet. Standing in front of him, I was met with the same story and the same excuses I'd heard all night. It hit me that nothing was going to change here. I left Mike's house feeling defeated, but as I walked away, something inside me stirred. It was on a pathway at Jaquith Park that clarity began to dawn. I could see my life for what it truly was: a series of empty, transactional relationships, all built on the shaky foundation of my addiction.

THE PAIN OF MISALIGNMENT

It was April 7, 2012, at 2 a.m., when the veil finally began to lift.

"The most terrifying thing is to accept oneself completely."
– Carl Jung

I saw myself clearly, perhaps for the first time. I had spent so many years pretending, hiding behind a mask of bravado and invincibility, but the truth was I was broken, lonely, and completely out of alignment with who I really was. I had been living a life of inauthenticity, chasing after things that didn't matter, ignoring the deep ache inside me that yearned for real connection, real purpose.

> *"Authenticity is the daily practice of letting go of who we think we're supposed to be and embracing who we are."*
> – Brené Brown

We all have a divine blueprint—a unique set of values, passions, and purposes that are meant to guide us. But when we live out of alignment with that blueprint, it creates a deep, gnawing pain. I had felt that pain for years but had tried to numb it with drugs, alcohol, and the high of risky behavior. The more I tried to escape it, the stronger it grew.

There's a profound misery that arises from refusing to confront the truth of who we are. We find ourselves trapped in a relentless cycle—filling the void with short-term fixes that never address the wound at its source. Misalignment gnaws away at our sense of worth and robs us of real peace. It hardens our hearts, poisons our relationships, and locks us in a perpetual state of striving without satisfaction. This is the agony of living at odds with our own design: a tension that no substance, no thrill, no amount of money, or fleeting companionship can truly relieve.

It's like Jesus said, "Therefore everyone who hears these words of mine and puts them into practice is like a wise man who built his house on the rock. The rain came down, the streams rose, and the winds blew and beat against that house, yet it did not fall because it had its foundation on the rock. But everyone who hears these words of mine and does not put them into practice is like a foolish man who built his house on sand." My life was built on sand. Everything I thought was solid—the drugs, the money, the friends—was crumbling, washed away by the storms I had invited into my own life.

THE EPIPHANY MOMENT

On that familiar pathway of Jaquith Park, I had a powerful realization. I was yearning for something deeper, something real. I wanted true friends, relationships that weren't based on what I could provide but on who I truly was. I wanted honesty, integrity, and connection. I wanted to make a difference in the world, to live a life that mattered. But I was so far from that vision it felt almost laughable.

Saint Teresa of Ávila once said, "It is foolish to think that we will enter heaven without entering into ourselves." I had spent so many years running from myself, hiding from the truth of who I was. I thought I could find fulfillment in the external—in substances, people, and status—but it was all empty. That night, as I walked away from Mike's house, I began to see that the real journey wasn't out there; it was within.

Realizing the path lay inward felt both humbling and terrifying. True change demanded courage not only to acknowledge the pain of misalignment but to choose a different way. To step forward, I had to admit that every shortcut I'd taken, every hollow escape I'd embraced, had led me further from the man I was meant to be. Such honesty hurts—it exposes the lies we've told ourselves and shatters the false image we've so carefully crafted. Yet, in that exposure, we discover a strange and unexpected gift: the beginning of genuine freedom.

Who looks outside, dreams; who looks inside, awakes
– Carl Jung

It was a profound awakening to the pain of misalignment between the life I was leading and the life I truly wanted. This epiphany was the beginning of a deep, internal transformation, a realignment towards authenticity and purpose that would reshape my entire existence.

I had to take off the mask I had been wearing for so long. I had to confront the lies I had told myself, the false identities I had created to survive. I wasn't Nick, the drug dealer, the addict, the criminal. I was Nick, the broken kid who longed to be loved and accepted for who he truly was.

"I did then what I knew how to do. Now that I know better, I do better."
– Maya Angelou

For the first time, I began to ask myself the questions that really mattered. Who am I? What do I truly value? What kind of life do I want to live? What kind of person do I want to be? These were questions I had avoided for so long, afraid of the answers, afraid of the pain that would come with facing them.

But I had to go there. I had to dig deep, to strip away the layers of pretense and lies, to find the real me underneath it all. It was terrifying. It was painful. But it was also liberating. I began to see that I wasn't just a product of my past or the sum of my mistakes. I was more than that. I had the power to change, to realign my life with my true values, and to become the person I was created to be. I did not know what that person was going to be, but I had an innate sense and clarity that who I was was not the person I was born to be. This awareness then made it possible to begin living and writing a new story for my life. A powerful revelation that exists in all of humanity.

THE ROAD TO INTEGRITY

Integrity is a word that gets thrown around a lot, but what does it really mean? At its core, integrity is about wholeness and honesty—living in alignment with our declared values and principles that define who we are. But what happens when you don't truly know what those values and principles are? When your actions can't align with your beliefs because you're not even sure what you believe in?

For years, I lived out of integrity—not because I wanted to deceive others, but because I was disconnected from myself. My life was a patchwork of contradictions, a series of actions that didn't match any coherent set of values. Deep down, I knew I had been raised with strong morals: hard work, kindness, the idea of loving thy neighbor. These principles were hardwired into me from my upbringing, but I had lost touch with them amid the chaos of my life.

Caught in the grip of addiction, I didn't know who I was or what I wanted. I couldn't articulate my values because I hadn't taken the time to discover them. My days were consumed with surviving the next moment, numbing the unbearable pain of disconnection. The more I ran from myself, the more out of integrity I became, and the deeper the void grew within me.

It wasn't just about saying one thing and doing another; it was about not knowing what to say or do in the first place. I realized that to find real freedom and live a life that mattered, I needed to reconnect with the core principles I had long ignored. I had to acknowledge that there was a standard—a moral compass—that I was inherently drawn to as a human being.

Rebuilding my life meant starting from scratch. I had to delve inward, uncovering the values buried beneath years of neglect and self-deception. It required facing painful truths and admitting that I didn't have all the answers. But with each step, I began to align my actions with the rediscovered beliefs that resonated with me. Brick by brick, I constructed a foundation rooted in integrity, even if I was still defining what that meant for me.

This inner realignment isn't just about choosing new actions; it's about daring to dismantle the entire framework of who we believed we were. When we decide to live by integrity, we're not simply adjusting our behavior—we're re-rooting our lives in soil that supports real growth. This shift calls us to face the discomfort of recalibration, to acknowledge all the ways we've fallen short, and to accept that healing won't be instantaneous. It's the ongoing courage to lean into the pain, knowing that true wholeness comes from embracing our honest reflection and daring to rebuild from the ground up.

Walking this path wasn't easy. It demanded honesty, courage, and the willingness to let go of habits and relationships that kept me anchored to my old self. But as I started to live in harmony with my emerging values, I felt a sense of wholeness I hadn't experienced before. I wasn't just surviving; I was becoming who I was meant to be.

Integrity became not just a concept, but a lived experience—a journey toward wholeness that began with the simple yet profound act of turning inward. By aligning my actions with my true values, even as I was still discovering them, I set the stage for a life of purpose and fulfillment. And in doing so, I took the first steps toward the freedom I had been seeking all along.

REBUILDING ON A NEW FOUNDATION

I started with the basics. Beginning from square one, I posed a fundamental question to myself: *What do I truly value?* It was a query I hadn't allowed myself to consider deeply before. In that season of my life, the answer emerged with unexpected clarity—relationships. Not just superficial acquaintances, but real, meaningful connections with people. I yearned to be honest, to live with integrity, to become someone others could trust. Deep down, I wanted to contribute something positive to the world, to make a difference, even if it was just in the life of one person.

Armed with this insight, I began to examine my life through

this new lens. Were my actions in harmony with these values? Were my relationships authentic, or were they merely transactional, built on convenience or mutual self-destruction? Was I living in a way that was true to myself, or was I simply playing a role that I thought others expected of me? More often than not, the honest answer was *no*. But instead of allowing this realization to crush me, I chose to see it as a starting point—a foundation upon which I could build a new life.

I knew change wouldn't come overnight, but I was determined to start somewhere. Cutting ties with those who kept me trapped was one of the hardest steps. I distanced myself from guys like Mike—the same Mike whose house I had walked away from on that pivotal night. Without any confrontations, I simply stopped talking to them, knowing they were unhealthy for me. I didn't want drugs and alcohol in my life anymore. Instead, I reached out to positive influences like Kevin, Ken, and Rhonda. I sought relationships that were healthy and challenged me to grow. Living with honesty was uncomfortable—I was so used to hiding—but it was liberating. I wasn't perfect and stumbled at times, but each time, I resolved to get back up and move forward, one deliberate step at a time.

Alongside reshaping my relationships, I realized I needed to address the spiritual void that had long haunted me. I turned to the Bible, not out of obligation, but out of a genuine desire for guidance and understanding. The stories of individuals who struggled and overcame resonated deeply with me. David's Psalms, in particular, spoke to my soul. His raw expressions of despair and his unyielding faith in the midst of turmoil mirrored my own internal battles. Reading his words, I felt less alone in my suffering. The accounts of the apostles also inspired me—ordinary men with flaws and failures who became pillars of faith and courage. Their transformations offered hope that change was possible, even for someone like me.

Seeking a supportive community, I began attending a local church. Walking through those doors for the first time was intimidating; I feared judgment and rejection. Instead, I was met with warmth and acceptance. People like Pastor Art and Trevor welcomed me without hesitation. They offered encouragement, guidance, and—most importantly—they listened. Through Bible studies and conversations over coffee, they helped me explore the values I wanted to embody. This body of believers became more than just a community; they became a family who encouraged, taught, and walked alongside me as I navigated this new path.

These changes weren't easy, and the journey was far from smooth. There were days when the weight of it all felt unbearable, moments when returning to my old life seemed tempting. But each time, I reminded myself of the freedom and purpose I was beginning to experience. By aligning my actions with my rediscovered values and surrounding myself with supportive relationships—both human and spiritual—I was slowly rebuilding my life. Brick by brick, step by step, I was constructing a foundation rooted in integrity—a life that not only mattered to me but could also make a difference in the lives of others.

In the quiet hours of forging this new life, I grappled with fears and doubts that tried to drag me back into old habits. There were moments when the ache of letting go felt almost unbearable—an emptiness that cried out for the familiar numbness of my past. But real freedom emerges when we push through that craving for comfort and into the territory of growth. Each decision to align with the values I uncovered was a small act of liberation, proof that one step at a time, we can transcend the very pain that once held us captive.

BUILDING A LIFE OF AUTHENTICITY

Authenticity isn't merely about being true to yourself; it's about being true to the person God created you to be. It's about aligning your life with the divine purpose woven into your very being—the unique calling that only you can fulfill. It's embracing every aspect of your journey—the good, the bad, and the messy—and recognizing each part as essential to your story and growth.

Saint Catherine of Siena said, "Be who God meant you to be, and you will set the world on fire." Those words ignited something within me. I wanted to spark that flame, to live a life that was bold, passionate, and genuine. I aspired to use my story—my pain, my struggles—to reach others who were lost and hurting, to show them that there is a way out, that hope is real and attainable.

But to light that fire, I had to start with myself. I needed to peel back the layers of inauthenticity, the masks I'd worn for so long, and stand bare before the truth of who I was. I had to accept myself, flaws and all, and begin to live in a way that was honest and aligned with the deepest values planted within me. It meant acknowledging that I was created in God's image, of infinite worth and value, with an intentional plan for my life—a purpose I was meant to discover and embrace.

This journey toward authenticity required courage. Letting go of the false identities I'd clung to wasn't easy. It meant stepping into the unknown, trusting that the person God intended me to be was worthy. I began to see that being authentic wasn't just about self-discovery; it was about aligning with the Truth—with a capital "T"—of what it means to be human, created for meaning and purpose.

As I embraced my true self, I found a newfound freedom. The more I lived authentically, the more my life began to make sense. I wasn't just existing; I was living with intention, with passion, with a sense of destiny. And in doing so, I was finally able to start setting my world on fire.

Looking back, I see that authenticity isn't a finish line to cross, but a continual process of choosing to express truth over illusion. It demands a willingness to confront pain points that, for so long, we've struggled to articulate. There is a raw, vulnerable beauty in this process—one that offers a deep sense of belonging and purpose. As we learn to stand firmly in who we are, our pain transforms from a silent thief into a teacher, guiding us toward the life we were always intended to lead. Each honest step forward becomes an offering of hope, not only for ourselves but also for those who will one day walk this path behind us.

I realized that authenticity and integrity are intertwined paths leading toward wholeness. By committing to live authentically, I was also choosing to live with integrity—aligning my actions with the values and purpose God had instilled in me. The journey was just beginning, but I was ready to step forward, embracing the person I was always meant to become.

YOUR UNBREAKABLE JOURNEY

1. Invitation to Reflection

> Find a peaceful place where you can be alone with your thoughts. Close your eyes and take several deep breaths, allowing tension to melt away with each exhale. Give yourself permission to be present in this moment, free from judgment or distraction. This is your sacred space for honest self-exploration.

2. Metaphorical Imagery

Imagine your life as a ship sailing the vast ocean. For a while, you may have been navigating through storms, your compass spinning wildly, leading you away from your intended destination. Today, you begin to realign your compass, setting a new course toward the horizon of your true self.

3. Guided Self-Inquiry

Where in your life do you feel a sense of misalignment or disconnection from your true self?

What masks have you been wearing to hide your authentic identity from others—and perhaps even from yourself?

What values or passions have you neglected that once brought you joy and fulfillment?

Take time to write down your responses, allowing your thoughts and feelings to flow without censorship. This is a journey, not a destination. The goal is to become curious, allowing you to shift if what you discover does not align with the kind of person you truly desire and commit to being in the world.

_____

_____

_____

_____

_____

4. Compassionate Engagement

As you uncover areas of misalignment, approach yourself with kindness and understanding. Recognize that every step of your journey has brought you to this point of awakening. Offer yourself the same compassion you would extend to a dear friend embarking on a path of self-discovery.

5. Deepening Awareness Exercise

Visualizing Your Authentic Self

Step 1: Close your eyes and envision yourself living a life that perfectly aligns with your deepest values and desires. What does a typical day look like? How do you feel as you move through this day?

Step 2: Write a detailed description of this vision. Include how you interact with others, the activities you engage in, and the emotions you experience.

Step 3: Identify the key elements from your vision that resonate most strongly with you. These are clues to your true self and what you value most.

6. Reframing Challenges

Acknowledge one significant area where you feel out of alignment.

Current Situation: Describe this aspect of your life honestly.

Example: "I am working in a job that doesn't fulfill me, and I feel disconnected from my passion for helping others."

Now, reframe this challenge as an opportunity for growth.

Opportunity for Realignment: Outline how you can begin to shift toward alignment.

Example: "I can explore volunteer opportunities or consider a career change that allows me to serve others at a high level and fulfill my passion."

_____
_____
_____
_____
_____

7. Incorporating Wisdom

Reflect on these words often attributed to the philosopher Socrates:

"To find yourself, think for yourself."

Consider how embracing your own thoughts, beliefs, and values can guide you back to your authentic path. Recognize that true alignment comes from within, not from external expectations or societal pressures.

8. Actionable Steps

Identify one practical step you can take this week to move toward realignment with your true self (and By-When date/time if applicable).

Possible Actions:

Begin a new hobby or revisit an old one that brings you joy.

Set boundaries in relationships that drain your energy.

Journal daily to deepen your self-understanding.

Your Chosen Action: Write down the specific step you will commit to taking.

_____
_____
_____
_____
_____

9. Personal Commitment

Craft a personal declaration to solidify your intention to live authentically.

Example: "I commit to honoring my true self by listening to my inner voice and aligning my actions with my deepest values."

Your Commitment Statement: Write your own declaration here.

_____
_____
_____
_____
_____

10. Vision of Empowerment

Close your eyes once more and envision the ship of your life sailing smoothly toward the horizon. Feel the wind guiding you, the sun warming you, and a sense of peace filling your heart. You are navigating with a clear compass now, aligned with your true north.

Hold onto this vision. Let it serve as a beacon, reminding you that every choice you make in alignment with your authentic self brings you closer to wholeness and fulfillment.

FINAL ENCOURAGEMENT

You are embarking on a courageous journey of self-realignment. Remember the wisdom of the poet Mary Oliver:

"*Tell me, what is it you plan to do with your one wild and precious life?*"

Your life is a gift, filled with potential and purpose that are uniquely yours. By seeking alignment, you honor not only yourself but also the impact you are meant to have on the world. Each step you take toward authenticity ripples outward, inspiring others to do the same.

EMBRACE YOUR JOURNEY

This exercise is more than a reflection—it's an active step toward reclaiming your true self. Revisit these prompts whenever you feel the pull of misalignment. Each time you choose integrity and authenticity, you strengthen your resolve and move closer to the life you are destined to live, accompanied by an exhilarating experience of freedom.

Remember, you are not alone on this path. As you align with your true self, you light the way for others to find their own.

Your journey toward freedom and purpose continues now.

THREE
THE CALL TO COURAGE
FACING FEAR AND FINDING YOUR TRUE PATH

God doesn't want us to be shy with his gifts,
but bold and loving and sensible.

THE MOMENT OF DECISION

At 2 a.m. on the morning of April 7, leaving Mike's house, I stood at a crossroads. For the first time in 12 years, I could see clearly. The fog of addiction and denial that had clouded my vision for so long was lifting, and I was confronted with the undeniable reality of my life. I could see the wreckage I had created, the baggage I was carrying, and the pain I had been trying so desperately to numb. But I also saw something else—hope. I glimpsed a future that could be different, a life that was not defined by my mistakes but shaped by the choices I would make from this moment forward.

Yet this promise of a new life didn't come wrapped in comfort or certainty. Instead, it exposed a raw vulnerability I had spent years trying to outrun. Every step toward hope seemed to magnify the fear lodged deep within my chest—a fear that perhaps I didn't have what it took, that I might stumble again, or that the world I was daring to imagine would never materialize. It was as if I stood on a narrow ledge, the ground of my old life crumbling behind me, and a vast expanse of the unknown stretching ahead. Would I find the strength to move forward, or would I cling to the only pain I knew?

"Hope is being able to see that there is light despite all of the darkness."
— Desmond Tutu

Two things were happening simultaneously. First, my eyes were opening to the fabricated, hollow life I had been living. Every lie I had told myself, every illusion I had built to protect me from the truth, was crumbling. Second, a new possibility was emerging on the horizon. I could see, just beyond my reach, the life I had always longed for—one of freedom, purpose, authenticity, and integrity. It was as if I had been handed a second chance, a blank canvas on which to paint a new story.

"Rock bottom became the solid foundation on which I rebuilt my life."
— J. K. Rowling

With this vision, however, came a wave of fear. Joy and hope were bubbling up, but so was terror. I didn't know if I had the courage to face my demons, to confront the pain, the trauma, and the suffering that had driven me to the brink. I had only known jails, institutions, and near-death experiences. Could I really do the work required to transform my life? Could I really face the broken pieces of my soul and begin the process of healing?

> "The only real prison is fear, and the only
> real freedom is freedom from fear."
> – Aung San Suu Kyi

As these thoughts swirled in my mind, I was making my way back to the house where I was staying. I had about six blocks to walk, and during that short distance, something incredible happened—something that changed the trajectory of my life forever.

THE ARREST THAT SAVED ME

I was arrested.

As I walked down the dimly lit street, I heard the sound of a car approaching. The spotlight flashed on, and a police officer's voice echoed through the still night air: "Nick!" I turned, and for the first time in a long time, I didn't feel anger, shame, or despair. I felt joy. Yes, joy.

I know how strange that sounds. But at that moment, as I stood there, caught red-handed with drug paraphernalia and facing yet another felony charge, I knew something profound. I knew deep down in my soul that I would never have to live that way again—not one more day. This arrest wasn't a setback; it was a turning point. It was the best thing that could have happened to me because it forced me to confront my reality in a way I had never done before.

I had told myself hundreds of times over the past 12 years that I would quit doing and dealing drugs, that I would turn things around, that I would do the right thing. But those promises were empty. I didn't believe them. I didn't believe in myself. This time was different. I knew it. Something had shifted. All of a sudden, I intrinsically knew or believed that a new, different version of living my life was available to me. I knew all along I could live a different life, as I had heard it over and over again in rehab, outpatient programs, and from my parents. But now I believed it deep in my heart. I shifted from knowing to believing this reality. I had finally reached the end of myself, and I was ready—truly ready—to change.

But readiness alone couldn't silence the trembling in my soul. Change demanded that I walk into uncharted territory without a map. I had to gamble on a future without the hollow comforts that once defined my existence. There were no guarantees, no promises that the path to freedom wouldn't break me before it remade me. Such uncertainty can tie our stomachs into knots, forcing us to confront how much we've come to rely on the very struggles we claim to hate. Courage, I realized, must be forged in the fires of our deepest apprehensions.

> *"When we are no longer able to change a situation, we are challenged to change ourselves."*
> – Viktor Frankl

THE COURAGE TO FACE THE PAIN

Courage isn't the absence of fear; it's acting in spite of it. At that moment, I realized that I had to summon a courage I didn't even know I had. I knew the road ahead would be hard, filled with challenges and obstacles that seemed insurmountable. I knew I would have to face the consequences of my actions, deal with my legal issues, and make amends for the damage I had caused.

But more than that, I knew I had to face myself. I had to go back into my story, revisit the wounds and traumas that had shaped my life, and start asking the hard questions: Why did I feel the need to be numb all the time? What was I running from? What pain did I truly have that I was unwilling to resolve? Why did I believe that I was worthless, broken, and defective? I had to dig deep to understand the roots of my addiction and begin the painful process of healing.

In this crucible of fear, I found unexpected inspiration from an ancient story a short time later—a moment in history when a leader named Joshua faced a daunting unknown. Charged with guiding his people into a new land, he stood on the brink of all he couldn't predict. Yet, a resounding command rang out: "Be strong and courageous." It acknowledged the terror of stepping beyond familiar borders while assuring him that he was not alone. This timeless encouragement, though spoken thousands of years before my crisis, felt startlingly relevant. If he could trust in a greater promise and press forward into unfamiliar terrain, perhaps I, too, could muster the resolve to confront my inner wilderness and move toward the life waiting on the other side of fear.

This kind of work isn't easy. It's messy, uncomfortable, and terrifying. But it's necessary. Without it, true transformation is impossible. You can't build a new life on the foundations of denial and avoidance. You have to tear down the old structures, examine the debris, and clear it away before you can begin to construct something new.

> "Owning our story can be hard but not nearly as difficult as spending our lives running from it. Embracing our vulnerabilities is risky but not nearly as dangerous as giving up on love and belonging and joy—the experiences that make us the most vulnerable. Only when we are brave enough to explore the darkness will we discover the infinite power of our light."
> – Brené Brown

THE DECISION TO BE COURAGEOUS

As I stood there, handcuffed and facing yet another stint in jail, I made a decision. In that stark moment, I resolved to face whatever came my way with courage. I would endure what I had to endure, confront what I had to confront, and do whatever it took to break free from the chains that had bound me for so long. Ironically, being arrested that night became the abrupt intervention I didn't know I needed—a harsh wake-up call forcing me to confront the reality of my life.

Something remarkable began to happen almost immediately. As backward as it might seem, going to jail became a resource—a turning point that set the stage for my transformation. In the weeks that followed, unexpected opportunities for growth, healing, and support started to flow into my life. After what felt like a thousand chances, my probation officer visited me before sentencing for the charges I faced that night. Instead of the condemnation I expected, she offered me another chance. She suggested I serve my six months of jail time at the Salvation Army Rehabilitation Center—a place where I could get clean, clear the fog, and engage in counseling and therapy while working 40 hours a week.

It was as if the universe had been waiting for me to make this decision, to take this step of faith, and once I did, doors began to open.

Yet deciding to embrace courage didn't mean fear evaporated overnight. Doubt still crept in, tempting me to return to what was known, even if it was destructive. The difference now was that I had a vision—however faint—of something worth fighting for. Stepping toward that vision required surrendering the illusion of control and allowing courage to guide me through unfamiliar territory. In these moments of trembling resolve, I learned that fear doesn't vanish; instead, it gradually loses its grip as we choose to advance in spite of it.

> *"When you want something, all the universe conspires in helping you to achieve it."*
> – Paulo Coelho

Embracing this opportunity, I immersed myself in the programs offered at the center. The days were long and challenging, filled with hard work and introspection. But as the weeks turned into months, I felt the chains that had held me begin to loosen. I was not just serving time; I was reclaiming my life.

Upon completing the program, I took another courageous step—I enrolled in community college at the age of 25, starting my journey toward a bachelor's degree. It was daunting to return to academics after so many years and being a high-school dropout, but I was determined to build a future I could be proud of. Simultaneously, I became deeply involved in Alcoholics Anonymous, surrounding myself with a community of people who, like me, were committed to pursuing a better life.

The Psalmist said, "Surely goodness and mercy shall follow me all the days of my life." I began to experience this in a very real way. As I made the choice to walk in courage, goodness and mercy truly followed me. People came into my life who supported and encouraged me—counselors, mentors, and fellow travelers on the road to recovery. Programs and resources became available that I never knew existed, each one helping me take another step forward. The path wasn't easy, and there were still obstacles to overcome, but I wasn't walking it alone now, which made all the difference.

Looking back, I realize that the moment I had chosen courage over fear, everything changed. The universe—or perhaps more accurately, God's provision—began to align in ways I could have never orchestrated on my own. By deciding to face myself and my circumstances head-on, I opened the door for transformation.

THE POWER OF TRUTH AND THE PATH OF TRANSFORMATION

One of the first steps in transformation is getting honest—truly honest—with yourself and those around you. It takes incredible courage to face the truth, to acknowledge your failures, your flaws, and your fears. We live in a world that is saturated with lies and distortions. Every day, we are bombarded with messages that tell us we need to be someone we're not, that we need to live up to some impossible standard. It's easy to get lost in that sea of deception in this upside-down world.

But truth is the currency of transformation. Without it, there can be no real change. Jesus said, "You will know the truth, and the truth will set you free." I had to start by telling the truth to myself. I had to acknowledge the reality of my addiction, my brokenness, and my need for help. I had to admit that I didn't have all the answers and that I couldn't do this on my own.

Once I began to walk in truth, once I started to strip away the lies I had believed for so long, I found a strength and freedom I never knew existed or that was possible. Truth is powerful. It cuts through the darkness, it dispels fear, it heals, and it empowers us to move forward with clarity and confidence.

> *"The truth is like a lion; you don't have to defend it.
> Let it loose; it will defend itself."*
> – Saint Augustine

COURAGE AS A CATALYST

Courage serves as the bridge between where you are and where you need to be, where you want to be, and where you were created to be. Without courage, the fear of failure, rejection, or discomfort can paralyze you, keeping you stuck in patterns that no longer serve you. Courage enables you to face uncomfortable truths, overcome limiting beliefs, and push through resistance.

The journey of transformation requires consistent, brave action in the face of uncertainty, discomfort, and fear. Whether it's in relationships, personal growth, health, or career, courage is the catalyst that propels you forward. It's the spark that ignites change, the fuel that keeps you moving when everything inside you wants to give up.

> *"Courage is the most important of all the virtues because without courage, you can't practice any other virtue consistently."*
> *– Maya Angelou*

I knew that if my life was going to transform, I had to cultivate this courage every day. I had to make a commitment to face my fears, to step outside my comfort zone, and to take bold, decisive action toward the life I wanted to create and the impact I wanted to make in the world around me. It wasn't easy. Every step felt like a battle, but with each victory, no matter how small, my courage grew.

PRACTICAL COURAGE: THE FIRST STEP

One of the best ways to begin building courage is to take one bold action every day that challenges your comfort zone. It doesn't have to be a grand gesture. It can be something as simple as having a difficult conversation, making a decision you've been avoiding, or starting a new habit. The key is to do something that evokes fear or discomfort—something that pushes you beyond the limits of your "safe" world.

Unfortunately, being human, when you take those actions,

you will undoubtedly choose and decide on something, and it won't turn out. You may even harm someone important to you as a result of practicing courage. Welcome, my friend. That is one of the most beautiful gifts and resource for you to get up and go again. To use the mistake and pain you created as an opportunity to reconcile, learn how to repent, make amends, restore, heal, and practice forgiveness. The beauty that becomes available when we fall down is nothing short of miraculous. You get to, in essence, graduate into another level of courage that was kickstarted from your initial decision to be courageous. It's messy. It's complex, but beyond worth it in every single way imaginable.

Think of it as strength training for your soul. Just as lifting weights builds physical muscle, taking courageous actions builds your courage muscle. Each small act of bravery began to stitch together a new identity in me. No longer defined solely by old wounds and regrets, I started to see myself as someone capable of weathering uncertainty. It was as if each courageous choice, each uncomfortable conversation, each newly embraced challenge, chipped away at the towering walls fear had erected in my mind. Day by day, I was proving to myself that I had the strength to step into the unknown. In doing so, I quietly reclaimed my right to live beyond the confines of who I had once believed myself to be.

The more you practice, the stronger you become. And as you strengthen your courage, you'll find it easier to confront the bigger obstacles in your life, to tackle the challenges that once seemed insurmountable.

> *"You gain strength, courage, and confidence by every experience in which you really stop to look fear in the face. You must do the thing you think you cannot do."*
> – Eleanor Roosevelt

EMBRACING THE JOURNEY OF TRANSFORMATION

Transformation is not a one-time event. It's a journey, a continuous process of growth, learning, and evolution. It's about becoming more of who you are, shedding the layers of fear and falsehood that have kept you small, and stepping into the fullness of your potential.

For me, this journey began with a single, courageous decision—to face the truth and to take responsibility for my life. It meant going back into my story, revisiting the pain and trauma that had shaped me, and beginning the work of healing and rebuilding. It meant embracing the discomfort, the uncertainty, and the fear, knowing, trusting, and believing that on the other side of that struggle was freedom.

Every day, I had to make the choice to be courageous, to step into the unknown, to confront the darkness within and around me. And with each step, I grew stronger, more resilient, more aligned with the person I was created to be. You can, too.

YOUR UNBREAKABLE JOURNEY

1. Invitation to Reflection

> Settle into a comfortable position in a quiet place where you won't be interrupted. Close your eyes and take several deep breaths, inhaling peace and exhaling tension. Allow yourself to be fully present in this moment. This is your safe space to explore your inner world with honesty and compassion.

2. Metaphorical Imagery

Imagine standing at the edge of a vast forest. The path before you is shrouded in mist, representing the unknown future. This forest symbolizes your fears and the challenges you must face to reach the life you desire. Today, you will take the first courageous step into this forest, trusting that each step forward brings you closer to your true self.

3. Guided Self-Inquiry

What fears are currently holding you back from pursuing the life you truly want? Take some time with this, as they probably don't show up as fear to you. Your brain is an expert at deceiving you. The fears may show up as impossibilities, so they don't register to you as possible to address.

How have these fears influenced your decisions and actions up to this point?

Recall a time when you acted courageously despite feeling afraid. What was the outcome, and how did it make you feel?

Write down your thoughts freely, without judgment or censorship.

_____
_____
_____
_____
_____

4. Compassionate Engagement

As you reflect on your fears, approach yourself with kindness and understanding. Acknowledge that fear is a natural response to uncertainty and that facing it is a brave and commendable act. Offer yourself the same encouragement you would give to a dear friend embarking on a challenging journey.

5. Deepening Awareness Exercise

Journey Through the Forest

Step 1: Visualize yourself stepping onto the path leading into the forest. Feel the ground beneath your feet and the cool air on your skin. What emotions arise as you take this first step?

Step 2: As you walk, obstacles appear—fallen trees, thick underbrush, shadows. Each obstacle represents a specific fear or challenge. Identify what each one potentially symbolizes in your life.

Step 3: Consider how you overcome each obstacle. Do you climb over, go around, or find another creative solution? What inner strengths do you draw upon?

Step 4: After navigating through the forest, you emerge into a sunlit clearing. Describe this place. How do you feel having faced and overcome the challenges along the way?

Document your journey in detail, noting insights and feelings that emerge.

6. Reframing Challenges

Identify one significant fear that you commit to address.

Current Fear: Articulate the fear honestly.
Example: "I fear that if I pursue my passion, I might fail and disappoint myself and others."

Now, reframe this fear as an opportunity for growth and transformation.

Empowering Perspective: Describe how facing this fear can lead to positive outcomes.

Example: "Attempting to pursue my passion, regardless of the outcome, allows me to grow, learn, and live authentically. Every experience enriches my journey."

_____
_____
_____
_____
_____

7. Incorporating Wisdom

Reflect on the words of author and motivational speaker Susan Jeffers:
"Feel the fear and do it anyway."

Consider how acknowledging your fear but choosing to act empowers you to move beyond limitations. Recognize that courage is not the absence of fear but the decision to move forward in spite of it.

8. Actionable Steps

Commit to one bold action this week that will help you confront your fear and advance toward your true path.

Possible Actions:

Reach out to someone who can support or mentor you to help you stay accountable.

Take the first step toward a goal you've been postponing.

Sign up for a course or workshop that challenges you.

Express your true feelings in a relationship or situation.

Your Chosen Action: Write down the specific step you will take (and By-When date/time if applicable)

_____
_____
_____
_____

9. Personal Commitment

Create a personal declaration to reinforce your commitment to courage.

Example: "I embrace courage by facing my fears and taking decisive steps toward my dreams. I trust in my strength and resilience."

Your Commitment Statement: Write your own declaration here.

_____
_____
_____
_____

10. Vision of Empowerment

Close your eyes and envision yourself one year from now, having consistently chosen courage over fear. Picture the achievements, the personal growth, and the fulfillment you've experienced. Feel the pride and joy that come from living authentically and bravely.

Hold onto this vision. Let it serve as a guiding light, motivating you to continue embracing courage each day.

FINAL ENCOURAGEMENT

You have taken a profound step by choosing to confront your fears and walk the path of courage. Remember the wisdom of philosopher Ralph Waldo Emerson:

"Do the thing you fear, and the death of fear is certain."

Every courageous act diminishes the power fear holds over you. Trust in your ability to navigate challenges, and know that each step forward strengthens your resolve and brings you closer to the life you desire.

EMBRACE YOUR JOURNEY

This exercise is a significant milestone in your journey toward a courageous and authentic life. Revisit these reflections whenever you need reinforcement or clarity. Remember, courage is a daily choice, and every time you choose it, you empower yourself further.

You are not alone on this path. Your courage not only transforms your life but also inspires others to find their own strength.

Your journey toward freedom and purpose continues now.

FOUR
THE POWER OF PURPOSE
FUELING A LIFE OF MEANING AND IMPACT

I know what I'm doing. I have it all planned out—
plans to take care of you, not abandon you,
plans to give you the future you hope for.

A few months after that life-changing night in April, I found myself in a place I never thought I'd be—sober, clear-headed, and experiencing something I hadn't felt in years: hope. It was July 7, 2012, and the oppressive summer heat was nearly unbearable. Yet, in the midst of that sweltering day, I experienced a revelation that changed the trajectory of my life forever. I had been clean and sober for three months—a milestone that felt like a lifetime. The fog of addiction and despair was lifting, and I was beginning to see the world and myself with new eyes.

For the first time in as long as I could remember, I was taking care of myself. I was sleeping well and eating properly, and my body was starting to feel healthy again. It was as if I had been asleep for years, and now I was slowly waking up, one layer at a time, to a reality that was both exhilarating and terrifying. The life I had been living was no longer an option. I knew that with every fiber of my being. There was no going back to the darkness, to the chaos and destruction that had once defined me.

But as I stood on the precipice of this new beginning, I was also gripped by a sense of uncertainty. I knew what I didn't want—my old life of addiction and pain—but I had no idea what lay ahead. Where was I going? What was I going to do with this newfound freedom and clarity? These questions swirled around in my mind, echoing off the walls of my newfound sobriety.

Then, on that blistering July day, the answer came. It was dramatic. It was shocking. It was laced with supernatural qualities. It was a resounding gong echoing throughout the halls, and at the same time, a gentle whisper. It came with a realization that my life had purpose, meaning, full of extraordinary possibilities. It was the first moment I saw with absolute clarity of what it means to be human and Who is in control, driving this thing called life. It was the moment that literally every single thing that I thought was true changed in an instant.

THE ENCOUNTER THAT CHANGED EVERYTHING

Looking back on my childhood, I realize how little I knew about God, faith, or spirituality. I didn't grow up in a church. I had no concept of who Jesus was or what the Bible said. The only interaction I had with God was through friends who attended a church youth group where they skateboarded—a pastime I loved and was passionate about. I thought it was cool that God could be associated with something I enjoyed, but that was the extent of my spiritual understanding.

Fast forward to that evening in July, and I found myself at a Celebrate Recovery meeting. It was there, in a room full of people who were also struggling and seeking healing, that something impossible happened. The God I had known only in passing whispers—the God who, in my mind, skateboarded—began to reveal Himself to me in a way that was deeply personal and undeniable.

He started to speak to me, not in an audible voice, but in a way that I could understand with such certainty. He showed me that He was the one who had set everything in motion, who had created the universe and everything in it, including me. He was the designer, the architect, the orchestrator of all things. And He made me Nick LeMonds for a particular journey to traverse while here on earth. I wasn't a mistake or an accident. I wasn't defective or broken beyond repair. I was created intentionally, purposefully, and beautifully by Him.

At that moment, I felt an overwhelming sense of belonging, of being seen and known in a way I had never experienced before. I realized that every experience, every mistake, every tear, and every triumph had been woven together into a tapestry that was uniquely mine. And at the center of it all was God, holding the threads, shaping the picture, and calling me to step into the life He had always intended for me.

Before this moment, I had been drifting through life like a ship lost at sea, lacking any meaningful navigation. Each encounter felt hollow, every conversation a passing formality, and each day blurred seamlessly into the next. I carried an ache deep in my soul—an emptiness I couldn't name but was desperate to fill. Without a guiding star, I stumbled into choices that only deepened the void. Now, as I stood in the wake of this encounter, it was as if a lighthouse appeared on the horizon, piercing through the fog that had obscured my vision for so long.

> *"I believe in Christianity as I believe that the sun has risen: not only because I see it, but because by it I see everything else."*
> – C.S. Lewis

A NEW BEGINNING: UNDERSTANDING MY WHY

At 7 p.m. that evening, with my heart pounding and my spirit raw and open, I encountered the living God in Christ. It wasn't a religious experience in the traditional sense—rigid, ritualistic, or bound by doctrines. Instead, it was profoundly personal, intimate, and deeply transformative. Religion, as I had known it, often felt like a set of rules and obligations, a box that tried to contain the uncontainable. But this encounter shattered those confines. It was relational, dynamic, and alive. I felt exposed and vulnerable, yet at the same time enveloped in a love and acceptance I had never known. It was as if God was saying to me, *"I see you, Nick. I know everything about you—every failure, every hurt, every secret—and I love you still. I am the One you have been searching for in the bottom of the bottle, pipe, baggy, and women. I made you. I am the One. I have made you for Myself, son. You're mine, all of you."*

He welcomed me with open arms, not with condemnation or judgment, but with a love that was pure and unconditional. In that moment, I connected with the very Source of all things—the One who had knit me together in my mother's womb. The weight of my past—the lies, the pain, the addiction—began to lift, replaced by a sense of freedom and hope. I realized that this was not about conforming to a set of religious expectations but about entering into a genuine relationship. He revealed to me that I was made to be loved by Him, to love Him in return, and to extend that love to others. That was my purpose, my why, the reason for my existence.

In the past, I had scoured the world for worth—trying to find it in substances, empty flirtations, and reckless escapades—yet nothing stuck. Without a reason for my existence, I had viewed my interactions as disposable and my future as a blank slate of uncertainty. But now, tethered to a truth far greater than my own understanding, I could finally see that every moment mattered.

Purpose acted like an inner compass, quietly but firmly pointing me toward a life where meaning infused the simplest of encounters and where each decision could lead toward growth rather than oblivion.

This revelation was both simple and profound. My purpose wasn't tied to a specific job, achievement, or status. It wasn't about following rules or fitting into a preconceived mold. It was rooted in a relationship—in being connected to the God who created me and reflecting His love in everything I did. This understanding was the foundation upon which everything else in my life would be built—a dynamic journey of ongoing discovery, meaning, and purpose.

> *"Being a Christian is less about cautiously avoiding sin than about courageously and actively doing God's will."*
> – Dietrich Bonhoeffer

BROAD AND NARROW PURPOSE

I like to think about purpose in two parts. You have a broad, overarching purpose, and a narrow underlying purpose, that can change and adapt in your day-to-day life. Think of your narrow as your assignments, given to you by God, that adjust over time as you live your life. The broad purpose is the overarching reason for our existence—the big picture of why we are here. When I had that profound encounter with God, I didn't grasp everything that was unfolding, but one thing became crystal clear: part of my purpose was to know this God who had reached out to me in such a powerful, tangible, life-altering way. To love and be loved by Him, to live a life that reflected His goodness and grace. This realization anchored me in a truth that transcended any understanding I had before. It was like discovering a compass pointing me toward a deeper relationship with the very Source of all things.

But there's also a narrow purpose, or your assignments, the specific ways in which we are called to live out that broad purpose in our daily lives. This is where our unique gifts, passions, and circumstances come into play. The narrow purpose evolves over time, shaping and shifting as God communicates specific assignments within the broad purpose. It's where the grand vision translates into tangible action—where loving God and loving people moves from an abstract concept to a lived reality. Every single thing I did—my interactions, my work, my relationships—became an opportunity to re-anchor myself to this profound, overarching purpose.

I began to see that every aspect of my life held significance within this framework. My marriage (one of my assignments) wasn't just about companionship; it was a sacred partnership where we could reflect God's love to each other and to those around us. Raising my children (one of my assignments) became more than just parenting; it was about nurturing souls entrusted to me and guiding them to discover their own purposes. My work (one of my assignments) was no longer merely a job; it became a platform to serve others, and to stand with humanity in meaningful ways. Even casual conversations with friends, family, and coworkers took on new depth as I sought to be present, genuine, and compassionate.

It struck me just how transformative genuine purpose could be. Before, I'd wandered through days feeling indifferent, as if I were a spectator in my own story. Now, each facet of life, from quiet moments to grand undertakings, felt charged with significance. Instead of chasing hollow thrills that left me emptier than before, I found myself inclined to invest in relationships, learning, and service. I no longer had to grasp at fleeting pleasures to feel alive; I had discovered a wellspring of meaning that flowed from my newly embraced purpose, quenching a thirst I never fully understood until it was finally satisfied.

Discovering my narrow purpose (or assignments), meant asking myself pointed questions: How can I use my unique experiences—my pain, my healing—to help others? In what specific ways can I take the freedom I've found and share it with those still trapped in darkness? What are the gifts and passions God has given me, and how can I employ them to serve and bless others? These weren't just theoretical musings; they became the driving force behind my daily decisions.

I realized that my past, with all its brokenness, was not a disqualifier but a tool. My journey through addiction and recovery equipped me with empathy and insight that I could use to reach others in similar situations. I started volunteering at local recovery programs, sharing my story in hopes that it might ignite hope in someone else. I sought opportunities to mentor, to listen, to simply be present for those who felt unseen. Standing with humanity became more than a phrase—it was a commitment to engage with the world in a way that was intentional and loving.

This understanding of purpose as both broad and narrow allowed me to navigate life with a renewed sense of direction. The broad purpose gave me an unwavering foundation—a reason for existence rooted in knowing and loving God. The narrow purpose provided the flexibility to adapt and respond to the specific needs and opportunities that arose each day. Together, they formed a cohesive framework that infused my life with meaning and impact.

Every action, no matter how small, became significant when viewed through this lens. Whether it was offering a kind word to a stranger, investing time in my children's growth, or collaborating with coworkers to achieve a common goal, I saw each moment as a chance to live out my purpose. Everything I did was an expression of the love I'd received, a way to reflect the grace that had so profoundly transformed my own life.

In embracing both the broad and narrow aspects of purpose, I found that life was no longer a series of disconnected events but a rich tapestry woven with intention and meaning. I wasn't just existing anymore. I was actively engaged with all parts of myself, experiencing a dynamic relationship between my Creator and the people in my world. And in that, I discovered a joy and fulfillment that surpassed anything I had ever known up to that point.

THE POWER OF PURPOSE IN ACTION

Having a clear sense of purpose is like possessing a compass that guides your life. It provides direction, clarity, and focus. It helps you navigate the challenges and obstacles that inevitably come your way because you know *why* you are doing what you're doing. You have a reason that is bigger than your fears, your doubts, or your circumstances that continually compels you forward.

Purpose is what propelled me forward during those early days of sobriety when everything felt uncertain and overwhelming. It gave me the strength to face my past, to make amends, and to start building a new life from the ground up. It reminded me that I wasn't just running away from something; I was moving toward something—something beautiful, meaningful, and real.

Viktor Frankl, a Holocaust survivor and renowned psychologist, wrote extensively about the importance of purpose in his book *Man's Search for Meaning*. He observed that those who were able to survive the horrors of the concentration camps were not necessarily the strongest or the healthiest, but those who had a reason to live—something to hold onto, a purpose that gave their suffering meaning.

Frankl's insights resonate deeply with my own journey. While my struggles were nowhere near the unimaginable horrors he endured, there were moments when the darkness felt overwhelming. In those times, it wasn't just about getting clean or staying out of jail; it was about finding a reason to live, something worth fighting for. Knowing my purpose gave me the courage to keep going, to face the pain and uncertainty with hope and resilience.

When setbacks arose, and old habits whispered temptations, it was my clear sense of purpose that fortified me against giving in. Understanding *why* I was on this path provided a well of strength to draw from when I felt weakest. Purpose and courage became intertwined; the clearer my purpose became, the more courage I found within myself to confront the battles ahead. This alignment between knowing my purpose and summoning the courage to live it out was crucial in overcoming the resistance and default wiring that had kept me bound for so long.

This infusion of meaning reshaped not only my inner world but also how I engaged with others. Conversations I once considered tedious or inconsequential suddenly held potential and weight. Where I used to feel detached and distant, I now sensed an undercurrent of connection. Purpose gave me the lens to perceive value in the people I encountered—a reminder that every interaction, no matter how brief, could leave a meaningful imprint on both our lives. What was once a barren landscape of trivial exchanges was now rich soil, ready to bear fruit through understanding, empathy, and kindness.

Purpose didn't eliminate the challenges, but it transformed the way I faced them. Each obstacle became not just something to endure but an opportunity to reaffirm my commitment to the life I was building. My purpose was the beacon that guided me through the storms, and the courage that arose from that purpose empowered me to keep moving forward, no matter how difficult the journey became, and trust me, there has been unfathomable difficulty along the way.

ALIGNING YOUR LIFE WITH YOUR PURPOSE

Knowing your purpose is one thing, but living it out is another. It requires intentionality, commitment, and a willingness to make difficult choices. It means aligning your actions, thoughts, and decisions with that purpose—even when it's hard, even when it's uncomfortable.

For me, this meant making changes in every area of my life. It wasn't just about avoiding old habits; it was about redefining who I surrounded myself with and where I invested my time. I had friends who still wanted to hang out in the same spots we always did—the dimly lit bars, the rundown houses where substances flowed freely, places that were familiar and deceptively comfortable. They'd call me up, saying, "Come on, just one night won't hurt." But I knew deep down that returning to those environments would pull me back into a life I was determined to leave behind.

Setting boundaries became essential. I had to have honest conversations—or sometimes, make silent decisions—to distance myself from relationships that no longer supported my growth. Letting go of these friendships felt like tearing away pieces of my own history. These were people I'd laughed with, cried with, and even considered family. However, I realized that if I wanted to honor my newfound purpose, I had to be willing to walk away from anything that didn't align with it or re-engage those people and places with different intentions, a sense of mission, to fulfill my purpose of loving God and others.

Making sacrifices extended beyond relationships. It meant dedicating time to go back to school, even when it felt overwhelming to sit in a classroom full of younger students. I spent countless hours reading, growing, and developing skills I never knew I had. Weekends that were once lost to escapades became opportunities for self-improvement and reflection. I traded nights out for nights in, pouring over books that expanded my mind and spirit.

There were moments when I had to put others' needs before my own desires—volunteering at local shelters, mentoring those who were walking paths similar to the one I had just escaped. These weren't obligations but choices that enriched my understanding of purpose. Each sacrifice, no matter how small, was a step toward the life I wanted to build.

Living out my purpose also meant being brutally honest with myself and others about who I was and what I stood for. I had to stop pretending, stop hiding behind facades, and start living authentically. This wasn't always easy. There were times when I stumbled, when I got off track, and when fear or doubt crept in. Old insecurities would whisper, *"Who do you think you are to change?"* But my purpose always brought me back. It was my anchor, my guide—the constant reminder of who I was and why I was here.

Embracing authenticity required daily courage. It was the practice of showing up as my true self, even when it felt vulnerable or exposed. But in doing so, I found a freedom I'd never experienced before—a liberation from the expectations and judgments that had once held me captive.

Standing on the other side of indifference, I realized just how draining it had been to live without direction. Before, I treated life as a series of distractions—anything to keep me from acknowledging the yawning emptiness within my heart and soul. Now, purpose served as my anchor, stabilizing me when my old fears resurfaced, and old temptations tugged at my sleeve. In embracing the authenticity that came with meaning, I had reclaimed agency over my story. Instead of drifting aimlessly, I pressed forward with intention and clarity, carrying within me a steadiness that no passing storm could easily erode.

> *"Authenticity is the daily practice of letting go of who we think we're supposed to be and embracing who we are."*
> — Brené Brown

FINDING YOUR OWN PURPOSE

You may not be at the same place in your journey. Maybe you're still searching for your broad purpose, trying to figure out who you are and why you're here. Maybe you were like me, who didn't know anything about God, wondering if He even exists and why I should care. That's okay. It's a process, a journey that unfolds over time. The important thing is to start asking the questions, to be open to the answers, and to be willing to explore the possibilities.

Purpose is not something you invent; it's something you discover. It's already there, woven into the fabric of who you are. It's in your passions, your experiences, your struggles, and your dreams. It's in the things that make you come alive, the things that break your heart, the things that you can't stop thinking about.

DEFINING YOUR PURPOSE

Purpose is not just a concept to understand; it's a reality to live out. I want to invite you to take some time to reflect deeply on your own purpose. Use the following exercise to help you gain clarity and direction. An exercise that, if engaged, could open up a brand new world to you. New hope. New impact. New legacy.

YOUR UNBREAKABLE JOURNEY

1. Invitation to Reflection

Find a quiet and comfortable place where you can be alone with your thoughts. Close your eyes and take several deep breaths, allowing your mind and body to relax. Let go of any distractions or concerns. This is your sacred time to explore the depths of your heart and uncover the purpose that fuels your life.

2. Metaphorical Imagery

Imagine your life as a book, and you are the author. Each chapter represents different phases of your journey, filled with experiences, challenges, and victories. Today, you hold the pen, ready to write a new chapter—one that is guided by a clear and compelling purpose. Envision the possibilities that unfold when you align your life with this deeper meaning.

3. Guided Self-Inquiry

What activities or experiences make you feel most alive and fulfilled?

What issues or causes are you most passionate about changing or supporting in the world?

Reflect on times when you felt a strong sense of purpose. What were you doing, and why did it feel meaningful?

What unique gifts, talents, or skills do you possess that can contribute to others' lives?

Allow yourself to write freely, capturing whatever thoughts and feelings arise without judgment. Give yourself permission to think big and dream out loud about what could be possible for your life. For your family. For your communities.

_____
_____
_____
_____
_____

4. Compassionate Engagement

As you delve into these questions, be gentle with yourself. Recognize that discovering your purpose is a journey, not a destination. It's okay if the answers aren't immediately clear. Trust that this process is unfolding perfectly for you, and honor every insight, no matter how small.

5. Deepening Awareness Exercise

Crafting Your Purpose Statement

Step 1: Review your responses from the guided self-inquiry. Look for common themes, passions, or desires that stand out.

Step 2: Write a draft of your personal purpose statement. This should be a concise sentence or two that encapsulates what you believe is your broad purpose in life.

Example: "My purpose is to inspire and empower others to overcome their challenges and discover their inner strength."

_____
_____
_____
_____
_____

Step 3: Refine your statement, ensuring it resonates deeply with you and feels authentic.

Step 4: Reflect on how this purpose can influence your daily actions and decisions.

6. Reframing Challenges

Identify any doubts or fears that arise when you consider living out your purpose.

Current Challenge: Articulate the fear or limiting belief.

Example: "I'm afraid I'm not skilled enough to make a real difference."

Now, reframe this challenge with an empowering truth.

Empowering Perspective: Offer yourself encouragement and a new viewpoint.

Example: "Every journey begins with a single step, and I can develop my skills as I go. My genuine desire to help is the most important starting point."

7. Incorporating Wisdom

Reflect on the words of motivational speaker Les Brown: *"You have greatness within you."*

Consider how this truth applies to you personally. Recognize that your experiences, talents, and passions equip you uniquely to fulfill your purpose. Embrace the idea that you are capable of making a meaningful impact.

8. Actionable Steps

Determine one specific action you can take this week to begin aligning your life with your purpose (and By-When date/time if applicable).

Possible Actions:

Volunteer for a cause you're passionate about.

Enroll in a course to develop a skill related to your purpose.

Reach out to a mentor or join a community group.

Start a project that reflects your passions and talents.

Your Chosen Action: Write down the action you will commit to taking.

_____
_____
_____
_____
_____

Compose a personal declaration to solidify your commitment to living out your purpose.

Example: "I embrace my purpose to [insert your purpose], and I commit to taking steps each day to bring it to life."

Your Commitment Statement: Write your own declaration here.

_____
_____
_____
_____
_____

10. Vision of Empowerment

Close your eyes and visualize yourself fully living out your purpose. See the positive impact you're making on others and how it brings fulfillment to your life. Feel the joy, passion, and sense of alignment that comes from embracing your true path.

Hold onto this vision. Let it inspire and motivate you as you move forward, reminding you of the meaningful difference you are making in the world.

FINAL ENCOURAGEMENT

You have taken a powerful step toward unlocking a life of true freedom and purpose and living an unbreakable life. Remember the wisdom of author Mark Twain:

"The two most important days in your life are the day you are born and the day you find out why."

Embrace your journey of discovery with excitement and courage. Your purpose is not a distant destination but a guiding light that illuminates your path each day. Trust in your unique gifts and the value you bring to the world.

EMBRACE YOUR JOURNEY

This exercise is a significant milestone in harnessing the power of your purpose. Revisit your purpose statement and action steps regularly, adjusting them as you grow and evolve. Remember, living with purpose is a dynamic journey that unfolds over time.

You are not alone in this endeavor. As you align with your purpose, you contribute to a greater tapestry of positive change in the world.

Your journey toward freedom and purpose continues now.

FIVE
FROM SETBACKS TO STEPPING STONES
BUILDING RESILIENCE THROUGH ADVERSITY

Consider it a sheer gift, friends, when tests and challenges come at you from all sides... so you will become mature and well-developed, not deficient in any way.

THE BIRTH OF RESILIENCE THROUGH FAILURE

Resilience isn't built in the comfortable, predictable moments of life; it's forged in the fire of adversity. It's sculpted in the crucible of setbacks, disappointments, and failures. This truth became a reality for me during one of the most challenging and humbling experiences of my leadership journey—a massive failure that turned into one of the most powerful growth opportunities of my life.

> *"Do not judge me by my successes; judge me by how many times I fell down and got back up again."*
> – Nelson Mandela

After discovering my broad purpose and setting my life on a new course, things began to fall into place. Within a year of that fateful evening on April 7, 2012, I found myself enrolled in community college, taking my first tentative steps toward a future I had never dared to dream of. Another year passed, and I was at a Bible college in Kansas, immersed in studies that I never imagined would captivate me the way they did. I graduated with a degree in Bible and Theology and moved to Southern California to pursue a Master of Divinity degree. By 2018, I was on the pastoral team at a large church in Orange County.

This was a miraculous transformation. Just six years before, I had been selling narcotics, drowning in addiction, and running from the law. Now, I was standing on a stage, sharing the Gospel and serving others. I had come so far, yet, as I would soon discover, there were still deep-rooted issues within me that needed healing.

THE PRESSURE OF LEADERSHIP

As I settled into my role on the pastoral staff, I was entrusted with increasing responsibilities. One of the most significant was organizing a large outreach event for our church—the International Food Festival. The vision was to bring together 20 families from our diverse congregation to share signature dishes from their home countries, creating a vibrant, multicultural experience for our church and the surrounding community. We planned for food booths, live music, bounce houses, dunk tanks, and kids' carnival games. It was set to be a remarkable event that required nearly 200 volunteers to execute successfully.

In the weeks leading up to the festival, I felt the weight of this responsibility more acutely than anything I had faced before. It was my first major leadership role, and I was determined to make it a success. But as the date approached, things started to unravel.

Volunteer after volunteer contacted me, saying they could no longer participate. Critical roles were left vacant just days before the event. It was overwhelming and, quite frankly, terrifying.

On the surface, I maintained my composure. I extended grace to each person who canceled, assuring them it was okay. "No worries, I understand," I'd say with a forced smile. But inside, I was spiraling. I was angry, frustrated, and overwhelmed with resentment. *How could these people be so inconsiderate? Didn't they know how much was riding on this event?* I felt like a victim—abandoned and alone, struggling to hold everything together.

I began to realize that my reactions were more than just stress-induced frustrations; they were signals of deeper issues within me. While I outwardly projected understanding, inwardly, I was harboring judgment and bitterness. I wasn't genuinely concerned about the volunteers or what might have caused them to back out. I didn't reach out to ask if they were okay or if they needed support. Instead, I silently cut them off, thinking, *Fine, if you don't want to help, so be it.* My focus was entirely on myself and the success of the event, not on the people I was supposed to be leading and loving, which was mind-blowing ironic!

This disconnect revealed significant holes in my leadership. I realized I didn't know how to manage my emotions or lead with genuine compassion. The very principles I professed—loving others, extending grace, being supportive—were absent in my actions. My inability to authentically care for my team was a glaring contradiction to the values I claimed to uphold.

THE BREAKING POINT

The event itself was a success. The food was delicious, the atmosphere was festive, and everyone seemed to be having a great time. On the outside, everything had come together beautifully. But for me, it was one of the most painful experiences of my life. Amidst the laughter and celebration, I felt a profound emptiness. I knew something was wrong—not with the event, but with me. Internally, I was in turmoil, and my shortcomings as a leader had been exposed in a way I wasn't prepared for.

At that moment, my mind swirled with a thousand questions: *Had I failed God's calling? Was I defective, incapable of loving people as I claimed I wanted to?* Underneath these fears simmered a realization—this disappointment could either define me as unworthy or refine me into someone stronger. The free will God had given me meant I had the power to choose which story I would tell myself. Would this setback crush my spirit, or could it become the very catalyst through which I learned to love more deeply, lead more compassionately, and grow more resilient than ever before?

Standing there among the guests, I felt isolated. The disconnect between my outward smile and inward struggle was tearing me apart. I had achieved the external success I wanted, but at the cost of my inner peace. I couldn't shake the feeling that I had failed—not in executing the event, but in leading with integrity and love.

The following Monday, during my scheduled meeting with the lead pastor, I couldn't hold back any longer. As soon as I sat down, the words poured out. I confessed the bitterness and resentment that had been festering inside me. I admitted that I wasn't handling the pressure well and that I felt completely out of alignment with the values I was supposed to be upholding.

"I've been so angry," I told him. "I acted like everything was fine, but inside I was seething. I didn't care about the volunteers—I only cared about the event's success. I didn't check on them or ask if they were okay. I just wrote them off. I feel like a fraud. Maybe I need help... perhaps therapy or something to understand why I'm reacting this way."

My pastor, to his credit, was incredibly supportive. He listened intently, his eyes reflecting empathy rather than judgment.

"Thank you for being honest," he said gently. "It takes courage to confront these feelings. Seeking therapy is a wise step. It's important to explore what's happening inside you."

His response was a relief. I had expected disappointment or criticism (which was another interesting story I was making up that was worth exploring), but instead, I found understanding and encouragement. It was a humbling moment but also a pivotal one. What felt like a leadership failure—my inability to manage my emotions and lead with grace—became the catalyst for a profound journey of self-discovery and healing.

I began to see that effective leadership isn't just about orchestrating successful events or achieving goals. It's about genuine connection, empathy, and the willingness to address one's own shortcomings. My frustration and anger weren't just personal issues; they were affecting my ability to lead others compassionately.

This experience taught me that leadership requires vulnerability and self-awareness. I needed to confront the uncomfortable truth that I was more focused on my own success than on the well-being of my team. I realized I had to learn how to manage my emotions, to be curious and supportive rather than dismissive. It was time to invest in understanding myself so I could become the leader—and the person—I aspired to be.

> "Leaders must either invest a reasonable amount of time attending to fears and feelings or squander an unreasonable amount of time trying to manage ineffective and unproductive behavior."
> – Brené Brown

THE JOURNEY INWARD

Two weeks later, I found myself in a therapist's office, beginning the process of exploring "the inner world of Nick LeMonds." I had no idea what to expect, but I knew I had to do something different. The bitterness and resentment I felt were symptoms of a deeper issue, and I was determined to get to the root of it.

Therapy was challenging in ways I hadn't anticipated. It forced me to confront parts of myself that I had long ignored or denied. I had to face the pain, the trauma, and the unresolved issues that had been driving my behavior for years. It wasn't easy. There were moments when I wanted to give up, when the discomfort of facing my own darkness felt too overwhelming.

But something incredible happened during those sessions. I began to see the patterns in my life, the cycles of behavior that had kept me trapped. I realized that my resentment toward the volunteers who had let me down was just the tip of the iceberg. Beneath it was a lifetime of unhealed wounds—feelings of inadequacy, fear of rejection, and a desperate need for control. This therapy journey was not just about fixing my leadership; it was about healing my soul.

"The wound is the place where the Light enters you."
– Rumi

THE SETUP OF A LIFETIME

In January of the following year, I enrolled in a class called Pastoral Counseling and Church Health. The timing couldn't have been better. The coursework and literature were focused on understanding human behavior, dealing with trauma, and providing compassionate care to those in need. It was as if every piece of information I was learning was directly applicable to my own life and healing.

As I dug into the material, I began to see connections between my personal struggles and the broader issues of leadership and ministry. I learned about the importance of self-care, the necessity of boundaries, and the power of vulnerability. I saw how my own unhealed wounds had impacted my ability to lead with authenticity and compassion.

This class, combined with my therapy sessions, set the stage for one of the most significant breakthroughs of my life. Little did I know that the universe was preparing me for something monumental—a revelation that would shake me to my core and change everything.

THE MEMORY THAT BROKE ME OPEN

It was early 2020, just before the world was turned upside down by the COVID-19 pandemic. I was lying on my bed, resting in the middle of the day, when a memory surfaced—a memory I had buried so deeply that I had forgotten it existed. It was a memory of trauma, of being molested as a young boy (a 7- to 8-year-old boy), of a violation so profound that I had blocked it out memory for over 25 years.

The memory hit me like a tidal wave, crashing over me with a force I wasn't prepared for. I was instantly overwhelmed with shame, guilt, anger, and confusion. How could I have forgotten something so significant? How had this trauma shaped my life, my choices, my relationships?

I was shaken to my core, but in the midst of the chaos, there was a strange sense of clarity. I realized that every step of my journey—the setbacks, the therapy, the counseling class—had been leading to this moment. I was being given an opportunity to confront this trauma, to process it, and to heal.

Here, in the raw aftermath of remembering my buried trauma, I stood before a choice. Suffering of any kind—whether it's the sting of failed leadership or the weight of old wounds—can seem senseless or cruel. But what if it was shaping me, chiseling away at my rough edges so I could better reflect the One in whose image I was created? I recalled how Scripture speaks of suffering producing perseverance, perseverance forging character, and character giving birth to hope. In facing these painful truths, I saw the faint outline of hope on the horizon—an unshakable assurance that no hurt was wasted when placed in God's hands.

> *"The best way out is always through."*
> – Robert Frost

TURNING THE SETBACK INTO A SETUP

It's often said that setbacks are setups in disguise, and this experience was no exception. What felt like a devastating blow was actually a doorway to freedom. I had the tools, the support, and the resilience to face this pain head-on. The therapy I was already engaged in provided a safe space to process the emotions and memories that were surfacing. The books I was reading gave me insight into the nature of trauma and the path to healing.

Over the next several months, I did the hard work of unpacking this trauma. I talked about it in therapy, journaled about it, and prayed through it. I allowed myself to feel the pain, to grieve the loss of innocence, and to forgive—not just the person who had hurt me but also myself for the ways I had responded to that pain.

This process wasn't easy, but it was necessary. It was a critical part of my healing and growth. I began to see how this unresolved trauma had influenced so many aspects of my life—my relationships, my self-worth, and my leadership. By facing it, I was able to break free from its grip and step into a new level of freedom and authenticity.

This shift in perspective felt radical. I had the freedom to interpret my struggles as evidence of my brokenness or as testimonies to the redemptive work happening within me. The trial that once taunted me as proof of my inadequacy now appeared as a training ground for becoming more like Christ. My setbacks didn't mean I was hopelessly flawed; rather, they revealed where healing and growth were still possible. Each disappointment now shimmered with the potential to shape me into a person of greater empathy, wisdom, and courage.

> *"You may not control all the events that happen to you, but you can decide not to be reduced by them."*
> – Maya Angelou

BUILDING RESILIENCE: THE POWER OF PURPOSE AND PERSPECTIVE

Resilience is not just about bouncing back from adversity; it's about learning and growing from it. It's about taking the setbacks that life throws at you and turning them into stepping stones toward your purpose. For me, the key to building resilience was staying grounded in my purpose and choosing to see every challenge as an opportunity for growth.

My purpose—to love God and to love people—became my anchor in the storm. It reminded me that no matter what happened, I could turn every negative experience into something positive. This mindset allowed me to extract meaning from every setback, to learn from every failure, and to keep moving forward even when the path was difficult.

When you are clear about your purpose, setbacks become less daunting. They are no longer obstacles to be feared but opportunities to be embraced. They are the fires that refine you, the chisel that shapes you, the wind that propels you forward. With each challenge, you grow stronger, wiser, and more resilient.

In this light, suffering becomes less of a punishment and more of a refining fire. Far from signifying a defective nature, adversity can illuminate the path toward transformation. When I embraced the truth that these hardships were not merely happening *to* me, but *for* me, my perspective shifted. I began to see suffering as an ingredient in the formation of unwavering hope—a hope that stands firm because it has been tested, purified, and proven true. This process was not a detour from my purpose, but a critical step along the journey toward a deeper faith, richer character, and fuller love.

> "Resilience is not just the ability to bounce back, but also the capacity to adapt in the face of challenging circumstances, whilst maintaining a stable mental wellbeing."
> – Dr. Carsten Wrosch

YOUR UNBREAKABLE JOURNEY

1. Invitation to Reflection

Find a peaceful place where you can sit comfortably without distractions. Close your eyes and take several deep, calming breaths. Allow yourself to be fully present in this moment. This is your time to explore your inner strength and resilience with kindness and honesty.

2. Metaphorical Imagery

Imagine yourself as a tree standing tall in a vast landscape. Over the years, you've weathered storms, harsh winds, and changing seasons. Each challenge has tested your strength but also deepened your roots. Today, you will explore how these storms have shaped you and how you can transform setbacks into stepping stones toward growth.

3. Guided Self-Inquiry

Reflect on a significant setback or challenge you've faced in your life. What emotions and thoughts arise when you think about this experience?

How did this setback impact your view of yourself and your abilities?

Can you identify any lessons or insights gained from this experience that have contributed to your personal growth? What were the lessons?

Write down your reflections freely, allowing yourself to express your true feelings without judgment.

_____
_____
_____
_____
_____

4. Compassionate Engagement

As you revisit this challenging time, approach yourself with compassion and understanding. Acknowledge the courage it takes to face adversity and recognize that your reactions were a natural response to difficult circumstances. Offer yourself the same empathy you would extend to a close friend.

5. Deepening Awareness Exercise

Reframing Your Story

Step 1: Write a brief account of the setback, focusing on how it made you feel and the impact it had on your life.

Step 2: Now, rewrite this account from a different perspective. Highlight the strengths you demonstrated, such as perseverance, courage, or adaptability.

Step 3: Identify at least three positive outcomes or lessons learned from this experience.

Example: "This challenge taught me the importance of self-care and seeking support when needed."

Step 4: Reflect on how this new perspective changes your understanding of the event and its role in your personal development.

_____
_____
_____
_____
_____

6. Reframing Challenges

Identify a current challenge or setback you're facing.

Current Challenge: Describe the situation honestly.

Example: "I'm struggling with feeling inadequate in my new job role."

Now, reframe this challenge as an opportunity for growth.

Opportunity for Growth: Outline how this situation can help you build resilience and develop new skills.
Example: "This is a chance for me to learn and grow professionally. By embracing this challenge, I can expand my abilities and gain confidence."

7. Incorporating Wisdom

Reflect on the words of Napoleon Hill:
"Every adversity, every failure, every heartache carries with it the seed of an equal or greater benefit."

Consider how adopting a growth mindset can empower you to transform obstacles into opportunities. Recognize that while you may not control external events, you have the power to choose your response.

8. Actionable Steps

Determine one practical action you can take this week to build resilience and move forward (and By-When date/time if applicable).

Possible Actions:

Set a specific goal related to overcoming your challenge and create a plan to achieve it.

Engage in activities that strengthen your well-being, such as exercise, meditation, or creative pursuits.

Learn a new skill that equips you to handle similar situations in the future.

Your Chosen Action: Write down the specific step you will commit to taking (and a "By-when" to it).

_____
_____
_____
_____

9. Personal Commitment

Craft a personal declaration to reinforce your commitment to resilience and growth.

Example: "I acknowledge my strength and ability to grow through challenges. I commit to viewing setbacks as stepping stones toward a brighter future."

Your Commitment Statement: Write your own declaration here.

_____
_____
_____
_____

10. Vision of Empowerment

Close your eyes and envision yourself in the future, having transformed your setbacks into successes. See yourself standing taller, roots deeper, branches reaching higher—just like the resilient tree. Feel the confidence and wisdom you've gained through these experiences.

Hold onto this vision. Let it inspire you to face current and future challenges with courage and determination.

FINAL ENCOURAGEMENT

You have taken a meaningful step toward building resilience and embracing your journey of growth. Remember the wisdom of Albert Einstein:

"In the middle of every difficulty lies opportunity."

Your experiences, both the triumphs and the trials, are integral to who you are becoming. Trust in your capacity to adapt, learn, and thrive. Every setback is not an end but a new beginning—a chance to rebuild stronger than before.

EMBRACE YOUR JOURNEY

This exercise is a testament to your willingness to grow and transform. Revisit these reflections whenever you need reinforcement or a reminder of your inner strength. Remember, resilience is a skill that develops over time through facing and overcoming challenges.

You are not alone on this path. Your journey toward resilience not only empowers you but also inspires those around you.

Your journey toward freedom and purpose continues now.

SIX
FROM SELF TO SERVICE
DISCOVERING FULFILLMENT IN GIVING

*That is what the Son of Man has done: He came to serve,
not to be served—and then to give away his life
in exchange for many who are held hostage.*

THE SHIFT FROM SELF TO SERVICE

When I made the decision to change my life on April 7, 2012, I knew something had to give. I knew deep within that if I kept living the way I was living, I would end up in jail or dead. I knew I had to find a new way of being, a new path that would lead me to the life I longed for—a life of purpose, joy, freedom, and fulfillment. But what I didn't know was that this new path would lead me to something even more powerful than sobriety; it would lead me to the transformative power of serving others.

Looking back, I realize how small and suffocating my world had become when it was all about me. My tunnel vision narrowed every choice down to how it could benefit me—what I could gain, how I could avoid pain, how I could keep up appearances. It was like walking through life with blinders on, unable to see past my own wants and needs. In hindsight, that me-centered existence felt like a prison cell where I held the key but refused to use it. Little did I know that by turning my gaze outward and aligning with my greater purpose to love God and love others, I would step into a far wider world of connection, meaning, and authenticity.

All throughout my childhood, I was familiar with the concept of recovery. My mother was deeply involved in Alcoholics Anonymous (AA), and she would take me along to meetings almost every day. I didn't understand much of what was happening in those rooms as a child, but I do remember the atmosphere—the honesty, the vulnerability, the sense of community. People would gather in those rooms to share their struggles with addiction and relationships, and as I got older, I began to grasp the significance of what I was witnessing.

When I finally decided to get clean, I knew that AA could be a lifeline. I had seen it work for my mother and for countless others. So, I started going to meetings, often twice a day, immersing myself in the program and its philosophy. One of the foundational principles of AA is the belief that true transformation comes not just from overcoming your own addiction but from helping others do the same. The final step of the famous twelve-step program is about carrying the message to those who still suffer and practicing these principles in all our affairs. It's about getting out of your own head and your own struggles and focusing on how you can serve others.

"The best way to find yourself is to lose yourself in the service of others."
– Mahatma Gandhi

THE POWER OF GIVING

It might sound strange, but in those early days of recovery, I began to see that the key to a fulfilling life wasn't about what I could *get* but what I could *give*. This was a radical shift for me. For most of my life, I had been utterly self-centered. Everything I did was about me—my comfort, my needs, my wants. I manipulated, I used, and I lied to get what I thought I needed. I believed that by serving myself, I would find happiness, but all I found was emptiness and despair.

This self-centeredness was at the heart of my addiction. I was trying to fill a void with things that could never satisfy me. Drugs, alcohol, women, relationships—they all promised to numb the pain, but they never delivered. And the more I pursued these things, the more isolated and disconnected I became. My life was a spiral of selfishness, leading me deeper and deeper into darkness.

But in those AA meetings, I learned a new way. I learned that there was something profoundly healing about giving yourself to another person, about sharing your hope and your strength with someone who was struggling just like you. When I began to do this, something shifted inside me. I found a sense of fulfillment and joy that I had never experienced before. I discovered that the secret to living wasn't about getting more but about giving more.

"No one has ever become poor by giving."
– Anne Frank

DISCOVERING PURPOSE THROUGH SERVICE

I realized that I had been saved and set free, not just for my own sake, but for the sake of others. I knew that my story, my struggles, and my recovery could be a source of hope and strength for someone else. This was a profound shift in my understanding of purpose. My life was no longer just about surviving or even thriving for myself; it was about making a difference in the lives of others. It was about loving God and loving people, as Jesus had commanded. I understood that this love wasn't just an abstract feeling; it was an active, intentional choice to serve.

Jesus Himself set the ultimate example of this kind of service. He said, "The Son of Man came not to be served, but to serve, and to give His life as a ransom for many." In the upside-down kingdom of God, greatness is measured not by how many people serve you but by how many people you serve. This was a radically different way of thinking for me, but I knew it was the path I needed to take.

THE JOY OF HELPING OTHERS

As I began to embrace this new way of life, opportunities to serve started to appear. One day, I received a call from an old friend—someone I had once partied and used drugs with. He told me that he had seen the changes in my life and was desperate to make changes on his own. He asked if I would meet with him, and I agreed.

We began to meet regularly, going through literature, sharing our struggles, and supporting each other in our journeys. I found a deep sense of joy and fulfillment in those meetings. Watching my friend take steps toward healing and transformation was incredibly rewarding. I was no longer just living for myself; I was part of something bigger. I was playing a role in someone else's story, and that was profoundly meaningful.

I realized that my purpose was starting to make sense, and it wasn't just about me. It wasn't just about what I could achieve or how much I could grow. It was about how I could use my story, my experiences, and my gifts to help others. This realization transformed the way I saw myself and the world around me. I was beginning to understand that true fulfillment comes not from serving yourself but from serving others.

> *"Only a life lived for others is a life worthwhile."*
> – Albert Einstein

FROM SELF-CENTERED TO OTHERS-CENTERED

The shift from self-centeredness to others-centeredness is not an easy one. It requires a complete reorientation of your mind and heart. It means letting go of the belief that your needs and desires are the most important thing in the world and embracing the truth that there is greater joy in giving than in receiving.

For me, this shift happened gradually. It started with small acts of service—showing up to meetings, sharing my story, listening to others, and serving in my local church. As I continued to serve, I began to notice changes in myself. I was less focused on my own problems and more focused on the needs of others. I was less anxious, less angry, and less fearful. I was experiencing a freedom and a peace that I had never known before.

This shift wasn't just about playing a different role; it was about engaging life on an entirely different level. When my perspective revolved solely around myself, my problems loomed impossibly large, and my relationships felt hollow. Other people became obstacles or resources rather than human beings with their own dreams, hurts, and hopes. Letting go of that mindset was like lifting a veil—suddenly, I could see the world beyond my own fingertips. I realized that each person I encountered held a piece of the greater puzzle, and loving them, serving them, wasn't a burden but a gift that expanded my sense of purpose and set me free from the chains of self-obsession.

Serving others also helped me discover strengths and gifts I didn't know I had. I found that I was good at listening, encouraging, and empathizing. I found that I had a passion for helping people overcome their struggles and find hope. These gifts were always there, but I had been too wrapped up in my own pain to see them.

As I continued to serve, I began to see the ripple effects of my actions. The people I helped started helping others. The hope and strength I shared with them were multiplied as they shared it with others. It was like a chain reaction of transformation, and I was just one link in the chain.

> "Service to others is the rent you pay for your room here on Earth."
> – Muhammad Ali

THE TRANSFORMATION OF SERVICE

Serving others doesn't just transform the people you serve; it transforms you. When you give of yourself—your time, your talents, your energy—you are changed. You become more compassionate, more empathetic, more loving. You begin to see people not as obstacles or inconveniences, but as fellow travelers on the journey of life.

One of the most profound lessons I've learned in my journey is that we find ourselves when we lose ourselves in service to others. When we stop obsessing over our own problems and start focusing on how we can help others, we experience a shift in perspective. Our problems don't necessarily go away, but they lose their power over us. We gain a sense of purpose and freedom that can sustain us through the most difficult times.

This is one of the great paradoxes of life. In giving, we receive. In serving, we are served. In helping others heal, we find healing ourselves. This is the secret of transformation that so many people miss. They are so focused on fixing themselves that they never realize that the fastest way to transformation is to stop focusing on themselves and start focusing on others.

In the quiet spaces where I once brooded over my personal

struggles, I now found genuine curiosity about someone else's journey. My pain no longer isolated me; instead, it became a bridge that connected me with others who were hurting. By leaning into their stories, I gained a deeper understanding of the human condition and saw that I was never truly alone. The paradox was beautiful: the more I gave of myself, the more whole I became. It was as though my wounds, once a source of shame, became the very channels through which compassion and empathy could flow.

> *"It is one of the most beautiful compensations of this life that you cannot sincerely try to help another without helping yourself."*
> – Ralph Waldo Emerson

FINDING FULFILLMENT IN SERVING

Fulfillment is also a word that gets thrown around a lot, but what does it really mean? For me, fulfillment is about living a life that is aligned with your values and purpose. It's about doing work that matters, building relationships that are meaningful, and making a difference in the world around you.

I found fulfillment not in pursuing my own happiness but in helping others find theirs. I found joy not in getting what I wanted but in giving what I could. I found purpose not in achieving my own goals but in helping others achieve theirs.

This doesn't mean that I never think about myself or my own needs. Self-care is critically important, and there are times when we need to focus on our own healing and growth. But the ultimate goal of healing and growth is not just to feel better, but to be better—to be a better friend, a better partner, a better leader, a better human being.

As I aligned my life with the divine blueprint—loving God and loving the person right in front of me—I realized that true fulfillment isn't fleeting or fragile. Rather, it takes root deep in the soul, nurtured by the daily choice to see others as valuable and worthy of care. This grounding truth reshaped every moment, from casual conversations to significant commitments. Where once I felt trapped in my own shadows, now I moved freely in the light of purpose. The people I once overlooked became the very reason I pressed forward, growing more confident that my life, when poured out for others, truly mattered.

YOUR UNBREAKABLE JOURNEY

1. Invitation to Reflection

Find a quiet, comfortable place where you won't be disturbed. Close your eyes and take a few deep breaths, inhaling peace and exhaling tension. Allow yourself to settle into this moment, releasing any distractions or concerns. This is your time to explore the transformative power of serving others and how it can bring profound fulfillment to your life.

2. Metaphorical Imagery

Imagine your life as a river flowing through a vast landscape. When a river dries up, the surrounding land becomes dry and barren. But when it flows freely, it nourishes the earth, bringing life and vitality wherever it goes. Today, you'll explore how allowing your gifts and compassion to flow outward can enrich not only others but also yourself.

3. Guided Self-Inquiry

Reflect on a time when you helped someone else, no matter how small the act. How did it make you feel? What did you notice about yourself?

What unique gifts, talents, or experiences do you possess that could benefit others?

Are there areas in your life where self-focus might be limiting your ability to connect with and serve others?

Write down your thoughts honestly and openly, allowing yourself to delve deep into your feelings and insights.

_____
_____
_____
_____

4. Compassionate Engagement

As you reflect, approach yourself with kindness and understanding. Recognize that shifting from self-centeredness to serving others is a journey that requires patience and grace. It's okay to acknowledge any fears or reservations you may have. Offer yourself compassion as you consider new ways to open your heart to others.

5. Deepening Awareness Exercise

Creating a Personal Service Plan

Step 1: Identify Opportunities
Look around your community, workplace, or social circle. Where do you see needs that resonate with you? What causes or issues stir your passion?
Example: "I notice that the local food bank is seeking volunteers to help distribute meals."

Step 2: Align with Your Gifts
Consider how your unique skills and passions align with these needs. How can you contribute authentically?
Example: "I love cooking and could prepare meals or teach cooking classes at the community center."

Step 3: Set a Specific Action
Write down a tangible step you will take to begin serving in this area.
Example: "This week, I will contact the volunteer coordinator at the food bank to offer my assistance."

Step 4: Visualize the Impact
Reflect on how this act of service might positively affect others and yourself. Envision the ripple effect your contribution could have.
Example: "By volunteering, I can help provide nourishment to those in need and foster a sense of community."

_____
_____
_____
_____
_____

6. Reframing Challenges

Identify any barriers or concerns that might hinder you from serving others and reframe them as opportunities.

Current Barrier:
Example: "I'm afraid I don't have enough time to commit to volunteering regularly."

Reframe:
Example: "Even small acts make a difference. I can start by volunteering once a month and see how it fits into my schedule."

7. Incorporating Wisdom

Reflect on the words of Mother Teresa:
"Not all of us can do great things. But we can do small things with great love."

Consider how even the simplest acts of kindness, when done with love, can have a profound impact. Recognize that you don't need to wait for grand opportunities to make a difference—you can start right where you are.

8. Actionable Steps

Commit to one practical action you will take this week to begin serving others (and By-When date/time if applicable).

Possible Actions:
Offer assistance to a neighbor or colleague who may need support.

Volunteer your time or skills to a local organization or cause.

Reach out to someone who might be lonely or struggling and offer a listening ear.

Your Chosen Action: Write down the specific step you will take.

_____
_____
_____
_____
_____

9. Personal Commitment

Craft a personal declaration to solidify your commitment to serving others.

Example: "I commit to sharing my gifts and time to enrich the lives of others. Through serving, I open my heart and find true fulfillment."

Your Commitment Statement: Write your own declaration here.

_____
_____
_____
_____

10. Vision of Empowerment

Close your eyes and imagine a stone dropped into a still pond, creating ripples that extend far beyond the point of impact. See yourself as that catalyst—your acts of service sending out waves of kindness and compassion that touch countless lives. Feel the sense of connection and purpose that comes from knowing you are contributing to something greater than yourself.

Hold onto this vision. Let it inspire you to continue embracing service as a pathway to fulfillment and positive change.

FINAL ENCOURAGEMENT

You have taken a meaningful step toward discovering the joy and fulfillment that comes from serving others. Remember the wisdom of Albert Schweitzer:

"I don't know what your destiny will be, but one thing I know: the only ones among you who will be really happy are those who have sought and found how to serve."

Your willingness to give of yourself not only transforms the lives of those you serve but also enriches your own life in profound ways. Embrace this journey with an open heart, knowing that every act of kindness contributes to a brighter world.

EMBRACE YOUR JOURNEY

This exercise is not just a reflection—it's an invitation to live a life enriched by connection and purpose. Revisit these prompts whenever you need inspiration or encouragement. Know that your contributions, no matter how small they may seem, have the power to create meaningful change.

You are not alone on this path. As you step into service, you join a community of people committed to making a difference, one act of kindness at a time.

Your journey toward freedom and purpose continues now.

SEVEN
LIVING IN HARMONY
INTEGRATING BODY, SOUL, AND SPIRIT

May God himself, the God who makes everything holy and whole, make you holy and whole, put you together—spirit, soul, and body...”

THE ALLURE OF EXTREMES

I've always been drawn to the extremes—testing my limits, rushing headlong into whatever caught my passion. From the outside, it might have looked bold and adventurous, but on the inside, it often led to fragmentation. I could be thriving in one aspect of my life—accomplishing big goals in ministry or deepening my spiritual insights—while simultaneously neglecting other vital areas. Maybe my spiritual growth was skyrocketing, but my physical health and emotional well-being were plummeting. I compartmentalized everything, boxing my life into separate categories that rarely interacted. Instead of working together as a unified whole, my body, soul, and spirit seemed to be pulling in different directions, leaving me feeling disoriented, scattered, and incomplete.

When I first came to know God in Christ, this tendency to live in extremes didn't go away; it just shifted focus. I went from having no spirituality to spiritualizing everything. My conversations revolved solely around my newfound faith, to the point where I was overwhelming others and isolating myself. I was so on fire for the things of God that I lost sight of the other parts of my life. I was compartmentalizing everything—my studies, my fitness, my relationships, my spiritual journey—all in separate boxes that never intersected. It was as if each part of me existed in its own isolated world, disconnected from the rest, and I found myself struggling to find balance.

This fragmentation wasn't just a logistical problem; it was a deep spiritual one. My body, soul, and spirit were operating in silos, and my life felt disjointed and incomplete. I was spiritually engaged but physically unhealthy. I was mentally focused but emotionally disconnected. I knew I needed to find a way to harmonize these parts of myself, to bring them together into a cohesive, integrated whole.

> *"True balance and harmony come from embracing all parts of yourself and integrating them into a whole. It's not about choosing between spirit and body, but aligning them both to live a complete and fulfilled life."*
> – Richard Rohr

THE COST OF COMPARTMENTALIZATION

When I got married, I was at peak physical health—I exercised regularly, ate well, and felt strong. But as I threw myself headlong into pastoral studies, ministry responsibilities, and the constant demands of serving others, I gradually let my physical health slide. At first, it seemed like a small compromise: skip a workout here, grab some junk food on the run there. But those "small" compromises added up fast.

I gained weight, felt sluggish, and became increasingly self-conscious about my body. Behind the scenes, the enemy whispered lies: "You don't have time to care for yourself," "Your physical health doesn't matter," or "Just push through." The truth was, this neglect impacted every arena of my life. Without physical vitality, my mind was clouded, my emotions unstable, and even my spiritual sensitivity dulled. By buying into the lie that I should pour everything into serving others while disregarding my own well-being, I was unknowingly undermining my capacity to love, lead, and live with purpose.

The truth, though, was that neglecting my body had a ripple effect on every other part of my life. I gained 20–30 pounds almost overnight, it seemed, and with that came a host of negative emotions—self-doubt, shame, and a sense of defeat. I felt sluggish and less confident, and even my spiritual walk felt diminished. The lie I had bought into—that serving others was more important than taking care of myself—was costing me dearly. I was running on empty, and it was only a matter of time before I burned out.

The irony is that in neglecting my body for the sake of serving others, I was actually undermining my ability to serve effectively. When I didn't take care of myself physically, it affected my mental clarity, my emotional resilience, and even my spiritual vitality. I was bringing all this negativity into my work, into my relationships, and into my ministry. It was a stark reminder that true transformation is holistic—it involves every part of who we are, not just one or two areas.

"Take care of your body. It's the only place you have to live."
– Jim Rohn

THE IMPORTANCE OF INTEGRATION

It was during this time that I realized I needed to stop compartmentalizing my life. I needed to integrate my body, soul, and spirit into a harmonious whole. The Bible speaks to this kind of holistic living. "May God Himself, the God of peace, sanctify you through and through. May your whole spirit, soul, and body be kept blameless at the coming of our Lord Jesus Christ." This verse paints a picture of what it means to live with integrity and wholeness, with each part of the self working together in harmony.

Understanding the definitions of body, soul, and spirit helped me to see how these elements are interconnected:

> **Body**: The physical structure of the human being, the vessel that carries us through this world. It needs care, nourishment, and exercise to function optimally. It is the temple in physical form, which God dwells within.
> **Soul**: The seat of our emotions, our personality, our mind, and will. It's where we experience healthiness, happiness, and vitality. It's where we process our experiences and form our worldview. This is the place where we have agency to curate, to shape, to form, to grow, and develop character.
> **Spirit**: The immaterial, transcendental part of us that connects with the divine. It's our innermost being, the essence that communes with God. This is the godlike part of every human on Earth, with the divine ability to love others as God loves us. It is the part that dignifies and declares that every human being is worthy and valuable.

To live fully and authentically, I had to bring these three elements into alignment. I couldn't neglect my body in favor of my spirit or ignore my soul while focusing on my physical health.

They all had to work together, each one supporting and enhancing the others.

In our modern, upside-down world, it's alarmingly easy to drift into compartmentalization. We live in a culture of convenience and excess—hyper-processed foods, chronic busyness, and relentless mental stimulation that can leave our bodies neglected, our souls weary, and our spirits malnourished. This isn't just a health crisis; it's a spiritual one. There's an underlying battle for our attention, focus, and overall vitality.

If the enemy can keep us exhausted, disconnected, and ashamed of our bodies, we're less effective as instruments of love and truth. To resist these pressures, we must see our physical health as intertwined with our spiritual calling. Honoring our bodies isn't vanity—it's stewardship. When we choose wholesome foods, regular movement, adequate rest, and space for mental renewal, we're not just "getting healthy"—we're aligning ourselves with God's design, making ourselves more available and effective for the assignments He entrusts to us.

THE LIE OF "NOT ENOUGH TIME"

One of the most insidious lies we tell ourselves is that we don't have enough time. "I'm too busy to exercise." "I don't have time to eat healthy." "I'm too tired to pray or meditate." But the reality is that when we neglect one part of ourselves, it affects every other part. When I stopped taking care of my body, I felt it in my spirit and soul. I was more irritable, more anxious, and less focused. I was less present with my family and less effective in my ministry.

The lie of "not enough time" is a trap that keeps us stuck in a cycle of self-neglect and dissatisfaction. The truth is we always have time for the things that are important to us. It's not about finding more time; it's about prioritizing what truly matters. When I began to prioritize my physical health, making time for exercise and proper nutrition, I noticed a dramatic improvement in my overall well-being. I had more energy, more clarity, and more capacity to serve others effectively.

The evil one often uses food and physical neglect as tools to derail us from our purpose. Most of the food we have access to today is so processed and stripped of nutrients that it leaves us depleted, both physically and mentally. When we're not nourishing our bodies properly, it's almost impossible to function at a high level in other areas of life. Taking care of our bodies is not a luxury or an afterthought; it's a foundational part of living a purpose-driven life.

> *"Those who think they have no time for bodily exercise will sooner or later have to find time for illness."*
> – Edward Stanley

HARMONIZING BODY, SOUL, AND SPIRIT

Bringing my body, soul, and spirit into alignment was like tuning a three-stringed instrument. Initially, each string sounded fine on its own, but together, they produced discord instead of harmony. As I began to care for my physical health—choosing nourishing foods, exercising, and getting enough sleep—I found my mind growing sharper and my emotions more stable.

As I devoted intentional time to prayer, reflection, and Scripture, my spiritual core strengthened, guiding and empowering my choices. The synergy was undeniable. Rather than competing for my limited time and energy, each dimension of my being supported and informed the others. My body became a faithful ally instead of a burden, my soul more resilient and calm, and my spirit freer to commune with God. In this integrated state, I found new clarity about my purpose—to love God and love others—and

I moved through life more fluidly, less weighed down by shame or confusion.

This process of integration isn't always easy. It requires intentionality, discipline, and a willingness to be honest with yourself about where you're falling short. But the rewards are profound. When you bring your body, soul, and spirit into alignment, you experience a sense of wholeness and peace that is unlike anything else. You feel more grounded, more connected, and more capable of living out your purpose.

> *"True health is not just the absence of disease. It is an integrated, holistic state of well-being in body, mind, and spirit."*
> – Andrew Weil

THE DANGER OF FRAGMENTATION

Living a fragmented life—where different parts of yourself are disconnected and out of balance—leads to stress, dissatisfaction, and a lack of true fulfillment. It's like trying to drive a car with the wheels out of alignment; you can move forward, but it's a bumpy, frustrating ride, and you're more likely to veer off course.

This fragmentation can show up in subtle ways. You might be excelling at work but struggling in your personal relationships. You might be thriving spiritually but neglecting your physical health. You might be emotionally resilient but mentally exhausted. Each of these imbalances creates friction and tension in your life, making it difficult to experience true peace and joy.

The solution is not to swing from one extreme to the other, but to find harmony and balance. It's about integrating all the parts of who you are so that your body, soul, and spirit are working together in concert, supporting and enhancing each other. This is what it means to live with wholeness and integrity.

Be sure to start where you are. If body image insecurities have kept you trapped in cycles of shame or if the chaos of life has convinced you that health is a luxury, take one small, concrete step. Maybe that's committing to a 10-minute walk each morning, preparing one nourishing meal a day, or setting aside a quiet moment to breathe deeply and reconnect with God's presence. Each of these choices sends a powerful message to your entire being: "I am worth caring for. I am designed to thrive. I can align my life with my values."

Over time, these small acts of self-stewardship accumulate, transforming the way you see yourself and your place in the world. As you practice integrated living, you'll notice a deeper sense of peace, resilience, and fulfillment that can't be achieved by focusing on just one part of who you are.

"Man is not fragmented; his body and soul are one. Any disturbance in the body affects the mind and soul, and any disturbance in the soul reverberates throughout the body."
– Pope John Paul II

Integration isn't a one-time event; it's a continuous journey of recalibration. Our seasons change, and so do our needs. There will be moments when your spirit soars while your body lags behind, or times when your mind races ahead and your heart needs healing. Don't see these imbalances as failures—see them as invitations to pay attention and realign. When you understand that your calling to love God and love others is best served by caring for every part of your being, you'll approach self-care with humility and gratitude. This holistic embrace of body, soul, and spirit equips you to show up fully, to nurture life-giving relationships, and to serve with a compassion that flows naturally from a well-tended heart.

YOUR UNBREAKABLE JOURNEY

1. Invitation to Reflection

Find a quiet, comfortable space where you can be alone with your thoughts. Close your eyes and take several deep breaths, inhaling slowly through your nose and exhaling through your mouth. Allow any tension in your body to release with each exhale. Give yourself permission to be fully present in this moment. This is your time to explore the harmony of your body, soul, and spirit.

2. Metaphorical Imagery

Imagine yourself as a beautifully crafted instrument—perhaps a violin or a grand piano. Each part of the instrument represents an aspect of your being: body, soul, and spirit. When all parts are in tune and played together, they create a harmonious melody. But if one string is out of tune or a key is missing, the music loses its beauty. Today, you'll begin the process of tuning each part of yourself to create a symphony of wholeness.

3. Guided Self-Inquiry

In what ways do you imagine you could potentially be compartmentalizing your life—separating your body, soul, and spirit?

Are there areas where you feel out of balance or disconnected from yourself?

How has neglecting one aspect of your life affected the other parts?

What beliefs or excuses have you held onto that prevent you from integrating these parts (e.g., "I don't have enough time")?

Write down your thoughts honestly and without judgment, allowing yourself to uncover the truth of your experiences.

_____
_____
_____
_____
_____

4. Compassionate Engagement

As you reflect on these questions, approach yourself with kindness and understanding. Recognize that acknowledging areas of imbalance is a courageous step toward healing and wholeness. Offer yourself grace, knowing that this journey is not about perfection but about progress and integration.

5. Deepening Awareness Exercise

Creating Your Integration Plan

Step 1: Identify One Action for Each Aspect

Body: What is one practical step you can take to care for your physical health?
Example: "I will commit to a 30-minute walk three times a week."

Soul: How can you nurture your emotional and mental well-being?
Example: "I will set aside 15 minutes each day for journaling or meditation."

Spirit: What practice can deepen your spiritual connection?
Example: "I will dedicate time each morning for prayer or reading inspirational texts."

Step 2: Set Realistic Goals
Ensure that each action is achievable and fits into your daily routine. Small, consistent steps lead to lasting change.

Step 3: Schedule Your Actions
Write down when and how you will incorporate these actions into your schedule.
Example: "I will walk during my lunch break on Mondays, Wednesdays, and Fridays."

Step 4: Visualize Integration
Close your eyes and imagine how incorporating these actions will create harmony in your life. Feel the synergy between your body, soul, and spirit as they support and enhance one another.

6. Reframing Challenges

Identify any obstacles or excuses that might hinder you from integrating these practices.

Current Obstacle:
Example: "I feel too busy to add anything else to my schedule."

Reframe:
Example: "By prioritizing these practices, I will enhance my overall well-being, making me more effective in all areas of my life."

7. Incorporating Wisdom

Reflect on the words from the World Health Organization: *"Health is a state of complete physical, mental and social well-being, and not merely the absence of disease or infirmity"*

Consider how embracing this holistic approach can transform your life. Recognize that each aspect of your being is interconnected, and nurturing all three leads to a fuller, more vibrant existence.

8. Actionable Steps

Commit to implementing the integration plan you've created (and By-When date/time if applicable).

Your Commitment:
Write down the specific actions you will take for your body, soul, and spirit. Examples:

Body: "I will walk each day for 30 minutes minimum."

Soul: "I will practice mindfulness meditation for 10 minutes each morning."

Spirit: "I will read a chapter from the Bible or an inspirational book before bed each night."

_____
_____
_____
_____
_____

9. Personal Commitment

Craft a personal declaration to reinforce your dedication to living an integrated life.

Example: "I commit to nurturing my body, soul, and spirit in harmony. Through intentional actions, I embrace wholeness and live authentically."

Your Commitment Statement: Write your own declaration here.

_____
_____
_____
_____

10. Vision of Empowerment

Close your eyes and envision yourself living in complete harmony. See yourself energized, peaceful, and connected—each part of your being supporting the other. Feel the balance and fulfillment that comes from this integration. Imagine the positive impact this wholeness has on your relationships, work, and overall happiness.

Hold onto this vision. Let it motivate you as you take steps toward integrating your body, soul, and spirit.

FINAL ENCOURAGEMENT

You have taken a powerful step toward embracing and harmonizing wholeness in your life. Remember the wisdom of philosopher Lao Tzu:

"To the mind that is still, the whole universe surrenders."

By aligning all aspects of yourself, you open the door to profound peace, freedom and fulfillment. Trust in your ability to create harmony within, and know that this integration enhances every facet of your existence.

EMBRACE YOUR JOURNEY

This exercise is more than a plan—it's a commitment to honoring every part of who you are. Revisit these reflections regularly to stay connected to your intention. Remember, integration is an ongoing process that evolves as you grow.

You are not alone on this path. As you strive for harmony within yourself, you inspire others to seek balance and wholeness in their own lives.

Your journey toward freedom and purpose continues now.

EIGHT
ROOTED IN FAITH
BUILDING A LIFE THAT STANDS STRONG

And I ask him that with both feet planted firmly on love, you'll be able to take in with all followers of Jesus the extravagant dimensions of Christ's love. Reach out and experience the breadth! Test its length! Plumb the depths! Rise to the heights! Live full lives, full in the fullness of God.

THE NEW IDENTITY

On that sweltering July 7 night in 2012, something truly transformative happened beyond discovering my broad purpose. I was given a new identity and a new name, and I became a new creation in Christ. This wasn't just a minor adjustment or a slight redirection—it was a complete reformation of who I was, a fundamental shift in my very being. Everything changed. The way I saw myself, the way I related to others, the way I understood the world—it all began to take shape around this new identity.

This new identity was not something tangible that I could hold or see. I couldn't touch it or quantify it in any physical sense. It was something I could only perceive through faith. It was a reality that I had to accept, believe, and live out, even though I couldn't fully grasp it with my senses. According to the Bible, I was now a child of God, a son of the King. This new identity set me free—free from the chains of my past, free from the self-destructive behaviors that had defined me, and free to step into a future filled with hope and purpose.

Faith became the bedrock of my life. It was the foundation upon which everything else was built. Every decision, every relationship, every thought, and every action was now filtered through this lens of faith. This identity rooted me, grounded me, and gave me a sense of purpose and stability that I had never known before.

This new identity wasn't just a positive self-improvement plan; it was anchored entirely in Jesus Christ—the One through whom, for whom, and by whom all things were made. Suddenly, it became clear that there was nothing else to "get" in this world apart from Him. Every earthly goal or treasure paled in comparison to knowing Jesus, to walking in step with His purpose, and to living out the assignment(s) He has for me. If He created me, if He designed the very fabric of my being, then all my striving could find rest in the truth that I was chosen, cherished, and placed here for a reason. No failure, no past sin, no haunting shame could overrule the voice of the One who called me "mine."

"Let us not mind earthly things, but soar to heaven; for the new man is renewed by the Holy Spirit and formed after the image of God."
– John Chrysostom

UNDERSTANDING IDENTITY THROUGH FAITH

This new identity—being a child of God—is not just a theological concept or an abstract idea. It is a profound truth that has real implications for how we live. Think about it: if you're a parent, you know that there is nothing your children can do to make you stop loving them. Your love for them is unconditional, unwavering, and unbreakable. Even when they mess up, even when they make mistakes, your love remains constant. This is how God loves us, how He loves me.

As a father to two daughters and with a baby boy on the way, I know this love firsthand. My kids make mistakes all the time. They spill things, break things, and create messes that can be incredibly frustrating. But none of that changes my love for them. I would die for them in a heartbeat. Nothing they do could ever separate them from my love.

And if this is true for me, an imperfect human father, how much more true is it for God, our perfect Father? He calls me His child. He is my Creator, my Father, and I am His son. There is nothing I could do to separate myself from His love. Nothing. No mistake, no failure, no wrong turn could ever change His love for me.

If we truly believe this, think of the possibilities that open up. If the God of the universe calls us His own, then there is no limit to what we can achieve, no fear that can hold us back, no failure that can define us. This is the power of faith. It transforms the way we see ourselves and the world around us.

> "God loves each of us as if there were only one of us."
> – Saint Augustine

WALKING BY FAITH, NOT BY SIGHT

But living out this new identity requires faith. It requires us to walk by faith and not by sight. This means trusting in things we cannot see, believing in truths that we cannot prove with our senses, and stepping out in boldness even when we don't know what the outcome will be. Faith is the assurance of things hoped for, the conviction of things not seen.

When I first started following Jesus, my life was still a mess in many ways. I was sleeping with multiple women, smoking cigarettes, and using foul language. I was far from the person I knew God was calling me to be. But something inside me had changed. My spirit began to whisper that I was out of alignment, that the way I was living was not in line with my new identity. I started to feel convicted about my behavior. I began to sense that there was a higher standard to which I was being called.

"Faith is a dark night for man, but in this very way, it gives him light."
— St. John of the Cross

This was not about following a set of rules or checking off a list of religious obligations. It was about living in a way that was true to who I now was in Christ. It was about honoring this new identity, about living out the freedom and purpose that had been given to me. And that required faith—faith to believe that God was with me, that He was guiding me, and that He would give me the strength to live this new life.

Embracing this new identity in Christ meant letting go of the shame and self-accusations that had once defined me. The Scriptures declare that in Jesus, we are holy, chosen, and blameless—covered by His righteousness and fully equipped with every spiritual blessing. I had to come to terms with the fact that I wasn't defective, that I wasn't a cosmic accident. Instead, I had been crafted intentionally and placed where I was, in the body I had, in the community I knew, for a divine purpose. This meant that the voice telling me I would always be stuck, broken, or unworthy had to bow before the truth of God's Word. My old narrative was replaced with the reality that my life now revolved around a

Savior who redeems every wound and transforms every loss into something meaningful.

THE CALL TO LIVE BY FAITH

Jesus said, "In this world, you will have trouble. But take heart! I have overcome the world." This is a promise and an invitation. It's a promise that we will face difficulties and challenges (let that sink in), but it's also an invitation to live through feeling fearful and to trust that He has already overcome everything that stands in our way.

Living by faith means believing this promise in the midst of our struggles. It means trusting that God is with us, that He is for us, and that He is working all things for our good. It means stepping out of our comfort zones, facing our fears, and taking bold actions in the direction of our dreams.

When I started this book, I was terrified. I had to wrestle with the fear that no one would read it, that it wouldn't make a difference, that it would just be a collection of random thoughts on paper. But I had to believe that God had called me to write this book for a reason. I had to trust that He would use it to help someone, to inspire someone, to bring hope and encouragement to someone who needed it.

This is what it means to live by faith. It means stepping out, taking risks, and trusting that God will catch us when we fall. It means believing that He has a purpose and a plan for our lives, even when we can't see it. It means knowing that we are His children and that nothing can separate us from His love.

If God is truly for me, if He holds all power and authority, then what could stand against me? This question isn't a cliché—it's a lifeline. Faith reminds me that when chaos swirls and visions seem delayed, the God of creation is still writing my story. Jesus, who overcame death itself, stands with me in every challenge.

When life appears to be going "bad" or when I interpret circumstances as setbacks, faith lifts my eyes to the greater truth: God's plan is unfolding, even when it's not visible. The Savior who once walked on water and calmed the storms can certainly handle the turbulence in my life. This unbreakable assurance doesn't mean I'll never feel disappointed or confused, but it does mean that none of those feelings have the final say.

> *"Faith is to believe what you do not see; the reward of this faith is to see what you believe."*
> – Saint Augustine

FAITH AND IDENTITY: LIVING IN ALIGNMENT

Faith and identity are deeply connected. When we understand who we are in Christ, it changes the way we live. It changes the way we see ourselves and the world around us. It changes the way we interact with others and the way we approach challenges. Our identity in Christ gives us the confidence to step out in faith, to pursue our dreams, and to make a difference in the world.

But living in alignment with this identity requires intentionality. It requires us to constantly remind ourselves of *who* we are and *whose* we are. It requires us to take captive every thought that contradicts this truth and to replace it with the truth of God's Word. It requires us to surround ourselves with people who will encourage us, challenge us, and hold us accountable for living out our faith in love.

This is not always easy. There will be times when we doubt, when we struggle, when we fall. But faith is not about never making mistakes; it's about getting back up and trusting that God is still with us, that He still loves us, and that He is still working in our lives. It's about walking by faith, one step at a time, and trusting that God will lead us exactly where we need to go.

> *"Faith never knows where it is being led, but it loves and knows the One who is leading."*
> – Oswald Chambers

Knowing who I am in Christ also compels me to love and serve others fearlessly. If I'm fully loved, fully forgiven, and wholly embraced by the King of kings, then I can step out in boldness. I can pastor a church in my old hometown, where my past misdeeds are well-known, confident that my former identity as a dealer or an addict has been eclipsed by my new role as a shepherd of souls. I can write a book or launch a business without paralyzing fear because my worth isn't measured by success or failure. Instead, my entire life stands on the unshakable foundation of Jesus' love and calling.

His voice whispers, "I made you for this moment. Walk forward. Take risks. Trust that I will supply every need." Such faith isn't blind optimism; it's anchored in the living Christ, who has proven His faithfulness time and time again.

FAITH IN ACTION: STEPPING INTO THE UNKNOWN

Living by faith means stepping into the unknown. It means taking risks, pursuing dreams, and trusting that God will provide what we need when we need it. This has been true in every major decision I have made since that night in July 2012.

Becoming a pastor was a massive step of faith. I had to overcome my own doubts and insecurities. Who was I to be a pastor? I had spent years running from the police, selling drugs, and living a life of destruction. How could I possibly shepherd others? But I knew that God was calling me to this role. I knew that He had a plan for me, and I had to trust Him.

Starting a church in my hometown required even more faith. How could I, Nick LeMonds, the former drug dealer and addict, lead a church in the same town where I had once been known for all the wrong reasons? But I had to believe that God could redeem my past and use it for His glory. I had to trust that He could turn my mess into a message, my pain into a platform for helping others.

Every step I have taken since that first step of following Jesus has required faith. Becoming a husband, a father, an entrepreneur—all of these roles have stretched me beyond what I thought I was capable of. Each one has required me to trust God in new ways, to step out of my comfort zone, and to believe that He is with me, guiding me and equipping me for the task at hand.

"God is looking for people through whom He can do the impossible—what a pity we plan only the things we can do by ourselves."
– A.W. Tozer

From a coaching perspective, this faith-fueled identity shifts how we approach every decision and relationship. When we know we are held securely by Christ, we approach challenges differently. We no longer have to manipulate situations or people to feel secure. Instead, we can invest wholeheartedly in loving our families, uplifting our communities, and influencing our workplaces with authenticity. We serve humanity not out of desperation for approval, but out of the overflow of God's love within us.

This is the crux of an unbreakable life: not personal perfection or flawless execution, but a steady gaze fixed on Jesus, allowing His wisdom and strength to guide our every step. Our assignments—whether it's being a husband, a father, a mother, a friend, starting a church, mentoring someone, or stepping into a new entrepreneurial venture—become opportunities to manifest God's grace in real and tangible ways.

FAITH AS THE FOUNDATION OF RESILIENCE

Faith is not just about believing in God's promises for the future; it's also about finding strength and resilience in the present. When the storms of life come, when everything seems to be falling apart, faith is what keeps us grounded. It's what gives us the strength to keep going, to keep believing, to keep trusting that God is in control.

I've faced many storms since that night in 2012. There have been times when I've felt overwhelmed when I've questioned my calling, when I've struggled to see how God could possibly be working in my life. But every time, faith has brought me back. Faith has reminded me of *who* I am and *whose* I am. Faith has given me the strength to stand firm, to keep moving forward, and to trust that God is with me, even in the darkest moments.

"Faith may swim where reason sinks."
– Charles Spurgeon

BUILDING A LIFE THAT STANDS STRONG

Faith is the foundation of a life that stands strong. It's the rock upon which we build our lives, the anchor that keeps us grounded, the source of strength that enables us to persevere. A life rooted in faith is unbreakable. It's not immune to challenges, but it has the strength and resilience to face those challenges head-on.

To build a life that stands strong, we must cultivate our faith daily. We must make time to connect with God, to study His Word, to pray, and to listen for His voice. We must surround ourselves with a community of believers who will support us, encourage us, and hold us accountable. We must step out in faith, taking bold actions in the direction of our calling, even when we can't see the full picture.

YOUR UNBREAKABLE JOURNEY

1. Invitation to Reflection

>Find a quiet and comfortable place where you won't be disturbed. Close your eyes and take several deep breaths, inhaling peace and exhaling tension. Allow yourself to become fully present in this moment. This is your sacred time to connect deeply with your faith and explore your relationship with God.

2. Metaphorical Imagery

>Imagine your life as a majestic tree planted by a river of living water. Your roots dig deep into the fertile soil, drawing nourishment and strength from the source. The river represents God's unending love and grace, flowing continuously to sustain you. As storms come and winds blow, your deeply rooted faith keeps you steadfast and unshakable.

3. Guided Self-Inquiry

>**Reflect on Your Faith Journey**
>
>**Pivotal Moments with God:**
>Recall the significant moments in your life where you have felt God's presence or guidance.

When did you feel His comfort during a challenging time?

Have there been moments where your prayers were answered in unexpected ways?

Write down these experiences and the lessons you learned from them.

Example: "When I was struggling with loneliness, I felt God's presence during a quiet walk in nature, reminding me that I am never truly alone."

_____
_____
_____
_____
_____

4. Compassionate Engagement

As you reflect on your journey, approach yourself with kindness and gratitude. Acknowledge that your faith journey is unique and personal. Celebrate the ways God has been at work in your life, and be gentle with yourself regarding any doubts or struggles you've experienced along the way.

5. Deepening Awareness Exercise

Identify an Area of Fear or Doubt

Facing Your Struggles:
Consider one area in your life where you currently struggle with fear or doubt.

Is it related to your career, relationships, health, or spiritual life?

How does this fear or doubt affect your actions and decisions?

Write down this area and how you perceive it's holding you back.

Example: "I fear stepping into a leadership role because I doubt my abilities, which prevents me from using my gifts to serve others."

_____
_____
_____
_____
_____

Find a Scripture to Anchor Your Faith

Seeking God's Word:
Find a Bible verse that speaks directly to your area of fear or doubt.

Use a Bible or online search to find relevant scriptures.

Choose a verse that resonates deeply with you and brings you comfort or encouragement.

Write down the verse and commit it to memory.

Example: "Philippians 4:13: 'I can do all things through Christ who strengthens me.'"
Reflect on how this scripture speaks to your situation and how it can help you overcome your fear or doubt.

6. Reframing Challenges

Transforming Fear into Faith:
Consider how viewing your challenge through the lens of faith changes your perspective.

How does trusting in God's promises alter your understanding of the situation?

What possibilities open up when you rely on His strength rather than your own?

Write down a new, faith-filled perspective on your challenge.

Example: "With God's help, I can step into leadership knowing He equips those He calls."

_____
_____
_____
_____

7. Incorporating Wisdom

Reflect on the words of Hebrews 11:1:
"Now faith is confidence in what we hope for and assurance about what we do not see."

Embracing Faith:
Contemplate how faith involves trusting in God's character and promises, even when circumstances are uncertain.

Recognize that many heroes of faith faced doubts and fears but chose to trust God anyway.
Allow this wisdom to inspire you to move forward confidently, knowing that God is faithful.

8. Actionable Steps

Take a Step of Faith

Putting Faith into Action:
Identify one practical step you can take this week to act on your faith in the area where you feel fear or doubt (and By-When date/time if applicable). Examples:
Having an honest conversation you've been avoiding.
Volunteering for a role that challenges you.
Letting go of a habit that hinders your spiritual growth.

Write down this step and set a specific time to do it.

Example: "I will speak with the director on Wednesday about serving in the upcoming outreach event."

_____
_____
_____
_____

Pray for courage and guidance as you prepare to take this step, trusting that God is with you.

9. Personal Commitment

Create a Faith Declaration

Affirming Your Identity in Christ:
Write a personal faith declaration that affirms who you are in Christ and your commitment to live by faith.

Include truths about God's love, your identity as His child, and your trust in His plans for you.

Example Declaration:
"I am a beloved child of God, chosen and redeemed through Christ. I am not defined by fear or doubt but by God's truth and grace. I will walk by faith, not by sight, trusting that Jesus guides my steps and strengthens me for every good work He has prepared for me."

_____
_____
_____
_____
_____

Read this declaration aloud daily as a reminder of *who* you are and *whose* you are.

10. Vision of Empowerment

Close your eyes and envision yourself living boldly in faith. See yourself overcoming the fear or doubt you've identified, stepping confidently into the actions you've committed to. Feel the peace and joy that come from trusting in God's promises and walking in alignment with His will.

Hold onto this vision. Let it empower you to face challenges with renewed faith, knowing that you are rooted deeply in God's love and purpose for your life.

FINAL ENCOURAGEMENT

You have taken a significant step toward deepening your relationship with God and embracing your identity in Christ. Remember the words of Isaiah 41:10:

"So do not fear, for I am with you; do not be dismayed, for I am your God. I will strengthen you and help you; I will uphold you with my righteous right hand."

Trust in His unwavering presence and let His promises be the foundation upon which you build your life.

EMBRACE YOUR JOURNEY

This exercise is not just a reflection—it's a step toward a more profound, faith-filled life. As you continue on this journey, remember that you are never alone. God is with you every step of the way, guiding, strengthening, and loving you unconditionally.

Continue to seek Him, trust in His plans, and walk boldly in the purpose He has set before you.

Your journey toward freedom and purpose continues now.

NINE
THE STRENGTH IN SOFTNESS
EMBRACING VULNERABILITY AS POWER

My grace is enough; it's all you need. My strength comes into its own in your weakness.

WRESTLING IN THE DARK

In the first year of Bible college, I found myself in the small town of Haviland, Kansas, grappling with a battle that threatened to tear me apart from the inside out. I was studying to become a pastor, immersing myself in the Scriptures, and preparing to shepherd God's people. Yet, despite all the growth and learning happening on the outside, there was a war raging within me—a struggle against my own carnal desires that seemed determined to suffocate and destroy me.

I was deeply entrenched in a hidden addiction to sexual images on the internet, a secret that gnawed at my soul and filled me with shame. Despite my best efforts, I couldn't seem to break free from its grip. I felt weak, ashamed, and trapped in a cycle of guilt and fear. It was the same suffocating darkness I had experienced when I was addicted to drugs and alcohol, but this time, I wasn't numbing my feelings. I was wrestling with them head-on, feeling every ounce of pain, anxiety, and frustration that came with this struggle.

Externally, everything seemed fine. I was excelling in my classes, serving in my community, and engaging in deep, meaningful conversations about faith and theology. But there was one area of my life that I kept hidden, one place that I didn't dare share with anyone else. It was the secret shame that stained every part of my life and prevented me from experiencing true freedom. I was living with a divided heart, pretending to be someone I wasn't, and it was tearing me apart.

> *"Shame derives its power from being unspeakable. If we cultivate enough awareness about shame to name it and speak to it, we've basically cut it off at the knees."*
> – Brené Brown

THE POWER OF CONFESSION

I knew that something had to change. I couldn't continue living this double life, pretending to be free when I was still in chains. One evening, during a Bible study with a group of guys on campus, I reached a breaking point. We had been meeting for several weeks, studying the Scriptures and sharing our thoughts and struggles. But up until that point, I had never shared the full extent of my battle.

Something inside me snapped that night. I couldn't keep hiding. I knew I needed to bring this darkness into the light, to expose the secret shame that was consuming me. So, with a trembling voice and a heart pounding with fear, I began to share my struggle. I told them about the addiction that was eating away at my soul, the shame that followed me everywhere I went, and the fear that I would never be free.

As I spoke, I felt the weight of my secret begin to lift. It was as if a huge burden had been taken off my shoulders. I was terrified, but I also felt an overwhelming sense of peace and relief. I had finally told the truth. I had finally let go of the pretense and allowed myself to be seen for who I really was. It took every ounce of courage I had to share that darkness with these men, but I knew in my heart that it was the right thing to do.

In that raw moment of confession, I experienced firsthand what Scripture promises: "If we confess our sins to one another, we will be healed." This isn't a formulaic ritual or a religious checkbox; it's an invitation to genuine honesty. Confession breaks the cycle of isolation and shame because it invites others into our reality. Rather than seeing confession through a lens of religious obligation, think of it as a powerful tool for personal growth and self-discovery.

As a coach, I've seen time and again how opening up—naming what's really going on beneath the surface—catalyzes transformation. When you speak the unspeakable, you strip shame of its secrecy and create space for truth to do its liberating work.

> "He who is alone with his sin is utterly alone. But it is the grace of the Gospel, which is so hard for the pious to understand, that confronts us with the truth and says: You are a sinner, a great, desperate sinner; now come, as the sinner that you are, to God who loves you."
> – Dietrich Bonhoeffer

VULNERABILITY AS A CATALYST FOR HEALING

What happened next was nothing short of miraculous. One by one, every single guy in that room began to share their own struggles with the same issue. I was stunned. I had felt so alone in my battle, convinced that I was the only one dealing with this particular sin. But here were these men, my brothers in Christ, admitting that they, too, were struggling with the very same thing.

At that moment, I realized something profound: vulnerability is contagious. By being willing to share my own brokenness, I had given them permission to do the same. It was as if a dam had burst, and all the shame and fear and guilt that we had been carrying began to pour out. We confessed our sins to one another, wept together, and prayed for each other. It was one of the most powerful, transformative experiences of my life.

That night, something shifted in our group. What had been a surface-level Bible study transformed into a community of true brothers, bound together by our shared struggles and our shared hope in Christ. We began to meet regularly, confessing our sins to one another, holding each other accountable, and supporting each other in our journeys toward healing and freedom. Vulnerability had opened the door to authenticity, and authenticity had opened the door to deep, meaningful connection.

> *"Vulnerability is the birthplace of love, belonging, joy, courage, empathy, and creativity. It is the source of hope, empathy, accountability, and authenticity. If we want greater clarity in our purpose or deeper and more meaningful spiritual lives, vulnerability is the path."*
> – Brené Brown

This transformation in our group wasn't accidental; it was the direct result of stepping into authenticity. In a world where so many people ache for genuine connection, your willingness to "go first" with vulnerability can ignite a chain reaction of honesty and healing. From a coaching standpoint, this moment illustrates a fundamental principle: authenticity breeds authenticity.

When one person dares to remove their mask, it grants permission for others to follow suit. Suddenly, what felt like a private prison of shame and struggle becomes a safe space where you realize you're not alone. And in that shared honesty, true freedom emerges—not just for you, but for everyone who steps forward into the light.

THE STRENGTH IN VULNERABILITY

Vulnerability is often misunderstood as a weakness, but in reality, it is one of the greatest strengths we possess. It takes incredible courage to be vulnerable, to open up and share the parts of ourselves that we would rather keep hidden. It requires us to embrace uncertainty, to risk rejection, and to face our fears head-on. But it is also the gateway to true healing and transformation.

When we allow ourselves to be vulnerable, we invite others into our story. We create space for genuine connection, for empathy, and for healing. We take off the masks that we wear to protect ourselves and allow others to see us as we truly are—flawed, broken, but also beautiful and worthy of love. This is the power of vulnerability. It breaks down walls, destroys shame, and builds bridges of understanding and compassion. It nearly always delivers the freedom *from* the source of the shame, and the freedom *to* then go and be light in the places we are created to go.

Jesus demonstrated this strength in vulnerability when He walked the earth. He wasn't afraid to show His emotions, to weep, to ask for help, to express His anguish. In the Garden of Gethsemane, He cried out to the Father, asking if there was any other way, and then submitted to the will of God, even though it meant suffering and death. His vulnerability wasn't a sign of weakness; it was a testament to His incredible strength and faith. He showed us that true power doesn't come from pretending to have it all together but from being willing to be real, to be honest, and to trust God even in the midst of our struggles.

Vulnerability also aligns you more closely with your divine

design. God didn't create you to operate behind walls of secrecy and fear; He formed you for relationship, transparency, and growth. Your faith journey isn't meant to be a solo climb; it's a communal ascent where each honest admission strengthens the bond among fellow travelers.

In a coaching context, this means your personal breakthrough becomes a resource for others. By shedding the facade of invulnerability, you invite people to encounter the real you—the one God shaped with purpose and potential. This authentic exchange not only deepens trust but also enhances your ability to love, serve, and lead with genuine empathy and courage.

> "Our brokenness is the wound through which the full power of God can penetrate our lives and unleash His grace. Our greatest strength lies in exposing our weaknesses to the healing grace of Christ."
> – Henri Nouwen

THE COURAGE TO TAKE OFF THE MASK

We all wear masks to some extent. We put on a brave face, a confident demeanor, or a smile to hide what's really going on inside. We pretend that we have it all together, that we're not struggling, that we're not hurting. But these masks don't protect us; they imprison us. They keep us isolated, disconnected, and alone.

Taking off the mask requires courage. It means being willing to admit that we don't have it all together, that we have struggles and fears and doubts just like everyone else. It means being willing to be seen, to be known, and to be loved—not for who we pretend to be, but for who we truly are.

In my own journey, I've learned that taking off the mask isn't just a one-time event. It's a daily practice, a continual choice to show up authentically in every area of my life. It's a commitment to being real, even when it's uncomfortable, even when it's scary.

It's a decision to live in the light, to reject the darkness of secrecy and shame, and to embrace the freedom that comes from being fully known and fully loved.

As you take off the mask and reveal the truth about your struggles, you become an active participant in your own story of redemption. Remember the lessons from earlier chapters: true freedom, purpose, and integrity form the backbone of an unbreakable life. Authenticity is the expression of these principles in action. By refusing to hide in shame, you allow Jesus—your Savior and guide—to work within you more completely.

Instead of "fixing" yourself in secret, you invite divine grace to flood those wounded places. Vulnerability, then, is more than an emotional release; it's a spiritual alignment. Through transparency, you position yourself to receive the healing, wisdom, and resilience that God has long desired to pour into you.

> "Vulnerability is not winning or losing; it's having the courage to show up and be seen when we have no control over the outcome. Vulnerability is not weakness; it's our greatest measure of courage."
> – Brené Brown

CREATING A CULTURE OF POWER AND STRENGTH

One of the most powerful things we can do as leaders, as friends, and as members of a community is to create a culture of subversive power and strength. This means fostering an environment where people feel safe to share their struggles, where they know they won't be judged or rejected, and where they can be real and honest without fear.

Creating this kind of culture starts with us. It starts with our willingness to be vulnerable, to go first, to set the example. When we are willing to share our own struggles and weaknesses, we give others permission to do the same. We create a space where people can let down their guard, take off their masks, and connect on a deep, authentic level.

In my own life, I've seen the impact of this kind of culture firsthand. I've seen how one person's willingness to be vulnerable can transform an entire community. I've seen how vulnerability can break down walls, heal wounds, and create connections that go far beyond the superficial. I've seen how it can change lives.

Taking the risk to be vulnerable isn't just about resolving a single struggle; it's about establishing a lifelong pattern of truth-telling and heart-sharing. From a coaching perspective, every time you choose to be honest about your weaknesses, you strengthen your capacity for personal growth and meaningful impact. Vulnerability becomes a cornerstone habit—one that permeates your leadership style, your family dynamics, your friendships, and your service to others.

This posture ensures that you're not just seeking temporary relief from shame, but building a foundation for ongoing transformation. You become a beacon of authenticity, inspiring others to embrace their own vulnerability and discover the unshakable strength concealed within their softness.

YOUR UNBREAKABLE JOURNEY

1. Invitation to Reflection

>Find a quiet, comfortable space where you won't be disturbed. Close your eyes and take several deep breaths, inhaling peace and exhaling tension. Allow yourself to become fully present in this moment. This is your time to explore your inner world with honesty and compassion, embracing vulnerability as a pathway to strength and connection.

2. Metaphorical Imagery

Imagine yourself standing in front of a mirror wearing heavy armor. This armor has protected you from hurt and rejection but has also isolated you and weighed you down. Today, you decide to remove each piece, feeling lighter and more authentic with every step. As the armor falls away, you see your true self—strong, beautiful, and worthy of love.

3. Guided Self-Inquiry

Identify Hidden Struggles:

What parts of yourself, at times, have you been hiding from others due to fear, shame, or vulnerability?

Is there a secret struggle, addiction, emotion, or aspect of your life you've kept hidden?

How has keeping these parts hidden affected your relationships and well-being?

Consider feelings of isolation, stress, or disconnection.

Write down your thoughts openly and honestly, allowing yourself to acknowledge these hidden aspects without judgment.

_____
_____
_____
_____
_____

4. Compassionate Engagement

As you reflect on your hidden struggles, approach yourself with kindness and understanding. Recognize that everyone has fears and imperfections. Acknowledge that vulnerability is a courageous act that can lead to healing and deeper connections with others.

5. Deepening Awareness Exercise

The Power of Confession

Step 1: Acknowledge Your Struggle
Write a letter to yourself describing the hidden struggle you've identified.

Express your feelings, fears, and how this struggle has impacted your life.

Step 2: Reflect on the Impact
How has keeping this struggle hidden affected your emotional and mental health?

Consider stress levels, self-esteem, and relationships.

Step 3: Sharing
Share this struggle with a trusted friend.

First, imagine the relief you would experience as a result of sharing. Picture the freedom of its weight off your shoulders.

As you prepare to share, what emotions arise? Relief, fear, hope?

6. Reframing Challenges

Transforming Vulnerability into Strength
Reframe vulnerability as a pathway to connection and healing rather than a weakness.

How can sharing your authentic self strengthen your relationships?

Consider the potential positive outcomes of being open.

Deeper connections, support, understanding.

7. Incorporating Wisdom

Reflect on the words of Brené Brown:
"Vulnerability is the birthplace of love, belonging, joy, courage, empathy, and creativity."

Embracing Vulnerability:
Contemplate how opening up can lead to richer, more authentic experiences.

Recognize that vulnerability allows others to see and appreciate the real you.

8. Actionable Steps

Taking the Courageous Step

Identify a Trusted Person
Who in your life do you feel safe with and believe would respond with compassion?

A friend, family member, mentor, or counselor.

Plan to Share
Decide on a time and place to have an open conversation with this person.

Ensure it's a comfortable environment for both of you.

Prepare Yourself
Consider what you want to share and how you might express your feelings.

Remember, it's okay to be vulnerable and take your time.

9. Personal Commitment

Create a Vulnerability Declaration

Write a personal declaration to solidify your commitment to embracing vulnerability.

Example:
"I choose to embrace vulnerability as a strength. I will courageously share my true self with others, knowing that authenticity leads to deeper connections and personal growth."

_____
_____
_____
_____

Read this declaration aloud to yourself, feeling the power of your commitment.

10. Vision of Empowerment

Close your eyes and envision yourself after sharing your vulnerability with someone you trust.

Feel the Weight Lifted
Imagine the relief and lightness that comes from releasing your hidden struggles.

Experience Connection
Visualize the supportive response from the person you've confided in.

Embrace Empowerment
Sense the strength and empowerment that arise from this courageous act.

Hold onto this vision. Let it inspire you as you take steps toward embracing vulnerability and authenticity in your life.

FINAL ENCOURAGEMENT

You have taken a brave and meaningful step toward embracing vulnerability and discovering the strength within you. Remember the wisdom of poet Maya Angelou:

"*We delight in the beauty of the butterfly, but rarely admit the changes it has gone through to achieve that beauty.*"

Your willingness to be vulnerable is a transformative journey that not only enriches your life but also encourages others to do the same.

EMBRACE YOUR JOURNEY

This exercise is a significant step toward living authentically and building deeper, more meaningful connections. Revisit these reflections whenever you need encouragement or clarity.

Remember, you are not alone on this path. Your courage to embrace vulnerability paves the way for others to do the same, creating a ripple effect of authenticity and compassion.

Your journey toward freedom and purpose continues now.

TEN
THE UNFINISHED JOURNEY
EMBRACING THE PATH OF ONGOING TRANSFORMATION

There has never been the slightest doubt in my mind that the God who started this great work in you would keep at it and bring it to a flourishing finish...

TRANSFORMATION IN REAL TIME

In the summer of 2018, I found myself in a class called *Pastor's Personal Life*, which was designed to help pastors integrate their faith and personal lives in a healthy, balanced way. Part of the course involved attending a training called *The Reveal*, a transformational experience that promised to challenge and reshape the way we saw ourselves and our ministry. Little did I know that this training would not only change my life but also become a cornerstone of my journey toward authentic living.

The Reveal was like nothing I had ever experienced. It was a vortex of transformation, a space where you couldn't hide from yourself. It was raw, intense, and powerful. From the very first session, my life began to shift in ways I couldn't have imagined. Before we even got past the ground rules, my entire worldview started to change. One participant, a woman who was struggling with a seemingly trivial rule, became the catalyst for this transformation.

The rule was insignificant in itself—you are not allowed to have your phone on in the training room—but it became a mirror reflecting all the unresolved issues and limiting beliefs she had been carrying. For nearly 20 minutes, the trainer—who would later become a mentor and friend—masterfully navigated her through layers of resistance, anger, and frustration. It was as if we were watching a master craftsman at work, gently yet firmly chiseling away at the walls she had built around herself.

What started as anger and frustration quickly escalated into an emotional storm. There was yelling, there were tears, there was deep anguish. And then, something extraordinary happened. As the trainer held space for her, refusing to let go of the truth, something within her shifted. The anger gave way to sorrow, the sorrow to relief, and then, almost miraculously, to laughter and joy. She was free. In that one moment, I witnessed the incredible power of truth and vulnerability. And as I watched her transformation unfold, something within me radically changed as well.

> *"All change is hard at first, messy in the middle, and gorgeous at the end."*
> – Tony Robbins

THE AWAKENING

That experience was like a bolt of lightning, illuminating the darkness of my own soul. I began to see the stories I had been telling myself, the lies I had believed, and the limitations I had placed on my own life. It was as if a veil had been lifted, and I could see clearly for the first time. The patterns and habits that had kept me bound and stuck were laid bare, and I realized that true transformation is not about a single breakthrough but about an ongoing process of shedding old skins and stepping into new realities.

I walked out of that training room feeling like I was on top of the world, filled with a renewed sense of purpose and possibility. I was on fire, ready to serve my community, my church, and my family with a new level of passion and commitment. But as time went on, the fire began to dim. I found myself slipping back into old patterns, falling into the same traps that had held me captive before—traps of low energy, low motivation, and disconnection from my purpose and my commitment to others.

It was frustrating and disheartening. I had tasted freedom, I had glimpsed the life I wanted to live, and yet here I was, back in the familiar territory of self-doubt and fear. I knew I needed to do something. I needed to reignite that fire, to get back into an environment that would challenge me and push me forward. So, I decided to return to another training with the same organization that had impacted me so deeply.

> *"When you change the way you look at things,*
> *the things you look at change."*
> *– Wayne Dyer*

THE CONTINUAL PROCESS OF TRANSFORMATION

This time, the experience was just as powerful. I walked out of that room with new dreams, new hopes, and new aspirations. I felt like a brand-new person, filled with courage, faith, and energy. But again, life happened. Challenges arose, obstacles appeared, and slowly but surely, I began to drift back into old habits and mindsets.

It was during this period that I realized something crucial: transformation is not a one-time event. It is an ongoing, never-ending journey. It is a process that requires constant attention, commitment, and effort. The Bible talks about moving "from one degree of glory to another degree of glory," and I began to understand what that meant on a deeper level. It's not about reaching a final destination but about continually growing, evolving, and becoming more of who you are meant to be. I am already glory, now, here, in real-time, with all my blemishes, with all my shortcomings, with all my mistakes. My goal is to keep transforming from one degree of glory to the next, and the next, and the next. Each degree having its own nuance, its own time frame, and its own needs.

This realization was both liberating and sobering. It meant that there would always be more work to do, more ground to cover, more layers to peel back. But it also meant that I could approach life with a sense of curiosity and adventure, knowing that each day offered new opportunities for growth and transformation.

> "I am the wisest man alive, for I know one thing,
> and that is that I know nothing."
> – Socrates

As I grappled with the idea that transformation never truly ends, I found solace and strength in the promise of Scripture. We are, at this very moment, being transformed "from glory to glory." This isn't a directive to become something we aren't, but rather to embrace and reveal more of who we already are in Christ. When God looks at us, He sees glory—He sees His beloved creation, already chosen, holy, and dearly loved.

The journey isn't about "fixing" ourselves or reaching some distant finish line of perfection. Instead, it's about steadily uncovering the glory that's already within, layer by layer, as we yield to His guidance and reshape our thinking according to His truth.

At the same time, this process demands that we no longer conform to the patterns of this world, but be transformed by the renewing of our minds. This renewal isn't a one-time event; it's a daily, sometimes moment-by-moment commitment. We must intentionally resist cultural narratives that glorify instant gratification, shallow success, and hollow identities. Instead, we choose to align with a higher vision—God's vision—knowing that every thought we bring into alignment with His truth moves us another degree into the fullness of who we are meant to be.

EMBRACING THE JOURNEY

Understanding that transformation is a lifelong journey has changed the way I live. It has shifted my focus from striving for perfection to embracing progress. It has taught me to be gentle with myself when I fall short and to celebrate the small victories along the way. It has shown me that every setback is an opportunity for a comeback, every obstacle a chance to learn and grow.

One of the most powerful tools I've found in this journey is staying connected to environments that foster growth. For me, that has meant immersing myself in transformational training, seeking out mentors and coaches, and surrounding myself with people who challenge and inspire me to be my best self. It has meant committing to ongoing learning and development, not just for the sake of achieving more, but for the sake of becoming more and serving others at a high level.

In the fast-paced, upside-down, ever-changing world we live in, adaptability and flexibility are essential. The world is constantly evolving, and so must we. With the explosion of information available at our fingertips, we have access to more knowledge than any generation before us. But knowledge alone is not enough. We must also have the wisdom to apply that knowledge in meaningful ways and use it to transform ourselves and the world around us.

> "Change is inevitable. Growth is optional."
> –John Maxwell

Part of embracing this ongoing transformation means refusing to let our emotions or circumstances dictate our direction. Feelings will ebb and flow, and life's storms will blow through unexpectedly. In these moments, having a clear, God-given vision acts as an anchor for our souls. Rather than living at the mercy of our moods, we live by the convictions that God has etched into our hearts. We choose joy when discouragement whispers in our ear, we choose love when apathy tries to creep in, and we choose faith when fear attempts to take the reins.

This isn't a matter of denying our feelings or pretending we don't hurt, struggle, or stumble. Instead, it's about acknowledging them without allowing them to lead. We trust the One who knows the end from the beginning, recognizing that we are in a process—sometimes messy, sometimes painful, but always with a purpose. Even when we fail to live up to our vision, we can get back up, relying on Jesus as our Savior in real time, renewing our minds with His promises and pressing forward in courage and grace.

THE COURAGE TO KEEP MOVING

The journey to authentic living requires courage—the courage to keep moving, even when the path is uncertain, even when we feel tired or discouraged. It requires us to keep pushing forward, to keep growing, even when it's uncomfortable. It requires us to embrace the unknown, to step into the mystery of who we are becoming, and to trust that the process will take us where we need to go.

There will be times when the journey feels overwhelming, when the obstacles seem insurmountable, and the temptation to give up is strong. But it is in those moments that we must dig deep, tap into our inner strength, and remind ourselves why we started this journey in the first place. We must hold on to the vision of who we are becoming and the impact we want to make in the world.

The journey to authentic living is not about achieving some perfect state of being. It is about being willing to show up, day after day, with an open heart and a willing spirit. It is about being willing to do the hard work of looking at ourselves honestly, facing our fears and insecurities, and taking responsibility for our own growth and development.

> *"Taking responsibility for your life is the foundation of everything you want to achieve. It's about owning your decisions, your actions, and your results, no matter how tough it gets."*
> – Tim Grover

THE ROLE OF COMMUNITY IN TRANSFORMATION

One of the greatest lessons I've learned on this journey is the importance of community. We are not meant to walk this path alone. We need each other. We need people who will stand with us, support us, and hold us accountable. We need people who will challenge us to be better, who will encourage us when we are down, and who will celebrate with us when we succeed.

In my own journey, I have been blessed with a community of people who have walked alongside me, who have seen me at my best and my worst, and who have loved me through it all. These relationships have been a lifeline, a source of strength and encouragement when I needed it most.

If you are on this journey of transformation, I encourage you to find your tribe. Seek out people who are committed to growth, who are willing to be real and honest, and who will support you in your journey. Surround yourself with people who inspire you, who challenge you, and who believe in you. These relationships will be invaluable as you navigate the ups and downs of this path.

"We are not meant to do this alone. Community is where we find strength, support, and accountability. It is in the presence of others that we discover our true selves and the courage to become who we are meant to be."
– Brené Brown

As we continue to evolve from glory to glory, it's essential to remember that we're not striving for unattainable perfection. We're practicing a lifelong dance of falling short and rising again, each time a bit stronger and wiser than before. This is precisely why we need a Savior, not just once, but every single day. Jesus stands ready to empower us with strength for the journey, grace for our missteps, and hope for the future. Our shortcomings don't disqualify us; they remind us how vital His presence is in our lives.

In this way, transformation becomes a celebration of progress rather than a lament over what still needs work. We acknowledge that we are already precious and glorious in God's sight, even as we eagerly anticipate the next degree of growth He has in store. By keeping our eyes fixed on Him, we ensure that each step we take—no matter how challenging—draws us closer to the fullness of life He intends for us. We learn to delight in the journey itself, knowing that as we lean on His strength and share the path with others, we are continually shaped into vessels of love, wisdom, and purpose.

YOUR UNBREAKABLE JOURNEY

1. Invitation to Reflection

Find a quiet, comfortable space where you won't be disturbed. Close your eyes and take several breaths, inhaling deeply through your nose and exhaling slowly through your mouth. Allow yourself to become fully present in this moment. This is your time to reflect on your personal journey and embrace the ongoing nature of transformation.

2. Metaphorical Imagery

Imagine your life as a path winding through a beautiful, varied landscape. Along the way, you encounter hills and valleys, sunshine and storms, but the path continues forward, inviting you to explore and grow. Today, you'll embrace this journey, recognizing that transformation is not a destination but an ongoing process of becoming.

3. Guided Self-Inquiry

Reflect on Past Transformations:
Identify significant moments in your life when you experienced personal growth or transformation.

What triggered these changes?

How did they impact your beliefs, behaviors, or perspectives?

Write down these experiences and the lessons you learned from them.

Example: "When I moved to a new city, I learned resilience and the ability to adapt to new environments."

_____
_____
_____
_____

4. Compassionate Engagement

As you reflect on your journey, approach yourself with kindness and understanding. Acknowledge that transformation often involves challenges and setbacks. Recognize the courage it takes to grow and the strength you've shown in navigating your life's twists and turns.

5. Deepening Awareness Exercise

Embracing Ongoing Transformation

Step 1: Identify Areas for Continued Growth
Consider areas in your life where you feel called to grow or change.

Is there a habit you'd like to develop or break?

A skill you'd like to learn?

A mindset you'd like to shift?

Write down these areas.

Example: "I want to become more patient and present in my relationships."

_____
_____
_____
_____
_____

Step 2: Acknowledge the Continuous Journey
Reflect on the idea that transformation is an ongoing process.

How does embracing this perspective affect your approach to growth?

Does it relieve pressure or create space for exploration?

Write down your reflections.

Example: "Understanding that growth is continuous allows me to be patient with myself and enjoy the journey."

_____
_____
_____
_____
_____

6. Reframing Challenges

Transforming Setbacks into Opportunities
Identify any fears or obstacles that might hinder your ongoing transformation.

What beliefs or thoughts are holding you back?

Reframe these challenges as opportunities for learning and growth.

Example*:* "Feeling uncertain is a sign that I'm stepping out of my comfort zone, which is where growth happens."

7. Incorporating Wisdom

Reflect on these words that are often wrongly attributed to author C. S. Lewis:
"Isn't it funny how day by day nothing changes, but when you look back, everything is different?"

Embracing Daily Progress:
Consider how small, consistent steps contribute to significant transformation over time.

Recognize that each day offers a new opportunity to grow and evolve.

8. Actionable Steps

Commit to a Growth Practice

Identify one practical action you can take this week to engage in your ongoing transformation (and By-When date/time if applicable).

Examples:
Start a daily journaling habit to reflect on your experiences.

Attend a workshop or webinar on a topic that interests you.

Set a small, achievable goal related to an area of growth.

Write down this action and plan when you will do it.

Example: "From 4:30–5:00 pm each night I will research until I find a workshop, class, or webinar that will teach me something."

_____
_____
_____
_____
_____

9. Personal Commitment

Create a Transformation Declaration

Write a personal affirmation that embraces the journey of ongoing transformation.

Example:

"I embrace the continuous journey of growth and transformation. I commit to being open, curious, and compassionate with myself as I evolve. Each day, I take steps toward becoming the best version of myself."

_____
_____
_____
_____
_____

Read this declaration aloud, feeling the commitment and openness to ongoing change.

10. Vision of Empowerment

Close your eyes and envision yourself walking along the path of your life's journey.

See yourself embracing each experience with openness and curiosity.

Feel the confidence and excitement that come from knowing that transformation is a natural and ongoing part of life.

Imagine the positive impact this mindset has on your relationships, work, and personal fulfillment.

Hold onto this vision. Let it inspire you to approach each day as an opportunity for growth and transformation.

FINAL ENCOURAGEMENT

You have taken a meaningful step toward embracing the path of ongoing transformation. Remember the wisdom of poet Rainer Maria Rilke:

"And the point is to live everything. Live the questions now."

Embrace your journey with patience and enthusiasm, knowing that each moment offers a chance to learn, grow, and become more authentically you.

EMBRACE YOUR JOURNEY

This exercise is an invitation to live fully engaged in the process of becoming. Revisit these reflections whenever you seek motivation or clarity. Remember, transformation is not a destination but a continuous path that enriches your life.

You are not alone on this journey. As you embrace ongoing transformation, you contribute to a world that values growth, resilience, and the endless possibilities of human potential.

Your journey toward freedom and purpose continues now.

ELEVEN
A MANIFESTO FOR AN UNBREAKABLE LIFE

In light of all this, here's what I want you to do... run on the road God called you to travel. I don't want any of you sitting around on your hands... And mark that you do this with humility and discipline—not in fits and starts, but steadily, pouring yourselves out for each other in acts of love.

It's late. The world outside your window has quieted, but inside, a war rages on. You've come so far, peeling back old layers, confronting illusions, daring to name your shame and reimagine your worth. You've confronted the masks you wear, faced down your fears, discovered purpose beyond self-interest, and learned that vulnerability isn't weakness, but the gateway to authentic strength. Now, as you stand on the brink of true freedom and lasting purpose, you may be wondering: "What now? How do I live this out, day after day?"

This is the moment to draw a line in the sand. To stake your claim. To decide—no matter how you feel, no matter what storms roll in—that you will live an unbreakable life. Not because you're perfect or because you've found some secret formula that smooths out every bump in the road, but because you know *who* you are, *whose* you are, and what you are here to do.

FREEDOM AND PURPOSE BEGIN WITH A DECISION

Let's be brutally honest: emotions can lie. Your heart, clouded by fear and scarcity, will sometimes whisper that you're not worthy—that your past defines you, that your weaknesses disqualify you, that your calling is too big a risk. There will be days when despair tries to tighten its grip, when shame growls from the shadows, when the old voices coax you back into numbness, retreat, and self-preservation.

But freedom isn't just the absence of chains; it's the refusal to let those voices dictate your life. It's choosing truth over feeling, courage over comfort. It's anchoring your identity in who God says you are, not the chatter of your insecurities. God didn't knit you together haphazardly; He fashioned you with loving intention long before you drew your first breath. You matter. You have a role to play that no one else can fulfill, a contribution to make that no one else can duplicate.

Purpose isn't a title or a trophy; it's a lens through which you view the world. It's the knowledge that your life, right here and now, participates in something infinitely meaningful—loving God, loving people, and walking out the assignments God places in your hands. It might be parenting your children through a tough season, pouring your creativity into a business that serves others, or mentoring someone who's lost their way. Purpose gives you direction when your feelings waver. Purpose steadies you when your emotions shout, "Quit."

CHOOSING VISION OVER FEELINGS

There will be dark nights of the soul. The Scriptures don't pretend otherwise. Jesus Himself warned, "In this world, you will have trouble." You will face financial strain, broken promises, shattered dreams, and unexpected losses. Betrayals may blindside you. Old habits may tug at your ankles like heavy chains. But here's the secret: You can feel all of it—sadness, anger, weariness—and still choose to stand up and go forward. You do not need to wait until you "feel ready." Readiness is a myth. Vision is what sustains you.

Without vision, people perish. Without a guiding star, you drift at the mercy of mood swings and cultural currents. But when your eyes lock onto a vision of who you are becoming—more loving, more courageous, more aligned with divine truth—your direction becomes clear. This vision might be as simple as: "I will be a person of joy, even when life cuts deep." It might say: "I will be the one who shows up, who speaks life, who doesn't withhold love." It might declare: "I will bring hope into every room I enter." Such vision propels you forward when exhaustion gnaws at your will. Vision, not feeling, leads.

CONDUCTING A "CSI" INVESTIGATION OF YOUR HEART

Sometimes the biggest barrier to living unbreakably free is the snap judgment we make about ourselves in the heat of struggle—like pronouncing ourselves guilty (or worthless) before weighing any actual evidence. You see this in every episode of a "CSI-type" TV show: a crime is discovered, and the investigators painstakingly gather evidence, test theories, and only after thorough analysis do they pin down the real culprit. The detective's cardinal rule is simple: don't assume—investigate.

Yet, as human beings, we often do the exact opposite. The moment we fail, face a betrayal, or miss the mark, we leap to condemning ourselves as defective or doomed. It's like deciding on a guilty verdict first and then cherry-picking every negative memory or harsh word to "prove" our case. Psychologists call this *confirmation bias*—a built-in tendency to favor evidence that supports the story we already believe ("I'm not worthy," "I am defective, flawed," "I always mess up") while ignoring anything that contradicts it.

But if you're going to stand firm in your God-given identity, you must become your own CSI detective. Suspend judgment instead of instantly pronouncing yourself the villain. Collect all the evidence—even the reminders of grace, support, past successes, and the truth of Scripture that declares you are fearfully and wonderfully made. Only then do you arrive at the truth of who you really are: not worthless or hopeless, but chosen, redeemed, and called with a purpose.

When you adopt this "CSI mindset" in moments of doubt, you break the cycle of self-condemnation and make room for the unshakeable vision God planted in you. And that vision, undergirded by real evidence of His faithfulness, is what will hold you steady when emotions try to mislead you into fear or despair.

THE INDISPENSABLE POWER OF LOVE

Love is the only game in town. When all is stripped away—status, possessions, reputation—what remains is love. Love that moves you to sacrifice for others, love that makes you bold enough to tear off your masks and reveal your true self, love that allows you to serve without fanfare or reward. Love that sends you back into the fray after a setback, determined to lift someone else up. Love that says, "I will not give up on people because God never gives up on me."

At the end of your life, you won't measure your worth by bank accounts or accolades, but by the love you offered and received.

People are the point. People are the prize. Those you influence, encourage, and nurture—these are the living legacies of your unbreakable life. Every conversation, every act of kindness or forgiveness, every time you pause to listen instead of judge, you are investing in the only commodity that truly lasts.

EMBRACE THE HARD TRUTH: STRUGGLE IS INEVITABLE

Let's not sugarcoat it. Struggle will come. Shame will try to choke your laughter. Insecurity will creep in at midnight. Some days, your heart will feel wicked and twisted, urging you toward bitterness, envy, or apathy. Your body may ache with stress, your mind with doubt. The enemy delights in your discouragement, in your retreat from boldness, in making you believe you're forever unworthy.

But none of that has the final say. When you're free, you acknowledge these hardships without letting them define you. When you're purposeful, you treat setbacks as stepping stones—imperfect, jagged stones, but stepping stones nonetheless. Press on. Resist despair. Remember that Jesus endured the cross for the joy set before Him—He looked past the immediate agony of the cross to eternal outcomes. Take the same stance. Your vision—the outcome you labor toward—will give you strength to face even the hardest moments.

YOU GET TO CHOOSE YOUR LEGACY

This is your life. You get to decide what experience people have when they're around you. Will they sense fear and guardedness, or welcome and warmth? Will they find cynicism or hope? Will they encounter a heart that, despite bruises, still chooses love?

You can't control every circumstance, but you can choose who you'll be in the midst of them. You can choose integrity over compromise. You can choose perseverance over resignation. You can choose to love hard, to give generously, to stand for truth when it's inconvenient. You can shape the atmosphere around you—an atmosphere of grace, understanding, and joy.

COMMIT TO THE PROCESS OF BECOMING

This isn't a one-time decision; it's a daily stance. You get up, you fail, you repent, you learn, you get up again. Over time, as you keep renewing your mind, grounding yourself in Scripture, your God-given vision, and leaning into community, you'll find that moments of weakness don't crush you like before. Shame's voice grows fainter. Fear's grip loosens. Not because you're superhuman, but because you're anchored in something unshakable: God's truth about who you are and why you're here.

God has been at work in you from the start, preparing good works for you to walk in, orchestrating a life that can reflect His love and creativity in countless ways. You are not an accident. Your story, with all its scars, can become a beacon of hope for others trapped in darkness. As you respond to Christ's invitation—"Come, follow Me"—you step into a divine partnership. He is the only One handing out new beginnings, fresh mercies, and the strength you lack. If you don't know Him, now is the time. If you do, renew your commitment. All freedom and all purpose originate and culminate in King Jesus. He is the wellspring of meaning, the fount of your identity, the anchor of every season.

COME HELL OR HIGH WATER, YOU HAVE DECIDED

Stand now. Decide who you will be. Determine that the life you've glimpsed on these pages will not remain theoretical. Yes, the night will get dark. Yes, problems will find you—financial strains, broken promises, shattered dreams, doubts, insecurities, and moments of feeling smaller than dust. But they do not have the final verdict.

You do not do this alone. Christ is with you, for you, and in you. Communities of honest hearts and truth-tellers surround you. The vision God placed in you burns quietly, ready to guide you when your heart misleads. Choose your life's story, chapter by chapter. Insist on joy, faith, courage, and love. Make it a non-negotiable. Write it into your soul's contract: "I will love, I will serve, I will grow, I will heal, and I will live free and purposeful, no matter what."

A FINAL CHARGE

You've learned what freedom looks like—honesty over pretense, truth over denial, love over isolation. You've learned what purpose feels like—serving a cause larger than ego, guided by an eternal calling. You know how to proceed—renew your mind, confess your struggles, embrace community, choose vision over emotion, and trust that God is continually unfolding your greatness, degree by degree.

Let your life testify that you have chosen light over darkness, authenticity over shame, resilience over despair, and love over everything else. When people meet you, let them encounter hope personified, truth embodied, and grace overflowing. This is an unbreakable life. This is the freedom and purpose you were born to live.

Now, step forward—unyielding, faith-fueled, heart-aligned. Come hell or high water, you have decided. This will be the life you forge, the legacy you leave, and the love you carry into every future dawn.

UNBREAKABLE DECLARATION: A VISION & COMMITMENT EXERCISE

1. Your Life, Your Arena

Close your eyes for a moment and imagine your life as an open arena—spacious, echoing with possibilities. Picture yourself stepping confidently into the center. Look around: who's in the stands cheering? What causes your passion? Where do you sense God's voice leading you forward?

Prompt: Name one specific area (family, career, ministry, personal growth) that you feel called to strengthen or transform.

_____
_____
_____
_____
_____

2. Craft Your "Victory Vow"

A vow is a concise, soul-level promise that captures your decision to stand unbreakably, even when emotions waver.

Example Format:
"I, (your name), stand today to declare that I will (key commitment), because I trust that God has (purpose or

reason). Come setbacks or storms, I remain unwavering in love, courage, and faith."

Prompt: Write your own vow in one or two bold sentences. Let it capture the **non-negotiable** line in the sand you're drawing.

_____
_____
_____
_____

3. Picture Tomorrow's Footsteps

Imagine waking up tomorrow already living by your vow. What's different about your mood, your conversations, and your approach to challenges? Who might you bless in this new posture?

Prompt: Describe in one or two paragraphs how tomorrow feels if you carry out this vow wholeheartedly. What small shift can you make right now—before you even close this book—to ensure you follow through?

_____
_____
_____
_____

4. Seal It With Intent

Finally, say your vow aloud—yes, out loud. Embody the words. Feel the weight of what you've declared. If possible, share it with someone you trust for accountability.

Prompt: Jot down a date you'll revisit your vow and reassess your progress. Circle it in your calendar, and let it be a reminder that you're in motion, forging forward.

Why This Matters
This isn't just a cerebral exercise. By crafting a "Victory Vow," **you're making a public stand**—even if that public is just you and God—against any old voices claiming you're stuck or disqualified. You're anchoring the truths of Chapter 11 in an act of **real-world commitment.**

You've read about living an unbreakable life; now you've spelled out a personal promise that **bridges** what you believe and how you'll behave. In essence, you've said, "Come hell or high water, I have decided." And that decision—rooted in your vow—becomes the **fuel** driving you to wake up tomorrow and live the calling you've just claimed.

CONCLUSION
EMBRACING THE UNFINISHED SYMPHONY OF TRANSFORMATION

Embracing. It's the act of stepping boldly into the arena of life, fully aware of the challenges yet undeterred by them. As we part ways in these pages, I want to leave you with a resounding truth: Your journey is just beginning. The transformation you've glimpsed is not a fleeting moment but an enduring call to live with unbridled freedom and purpose.

We've walked together through shadows and light, unraveling the threads that have woven your story thus far. Now, it's time to ignite the fire within, to harness the courage that propels you beyond the ordinary, and to unleash your authentic self upon a world that desperately needs it.

UNVEILING THE ENEMIES WITHIN

But be forewarned: there are adversaries that lurk within—subtle yet potent forces that seek to hinder your ascent. Recognizing and overcoming these four enemies is crucial to living the life you were destined for, an unbreakable life filled with freedom and purpose.

THE NEED TO BE RIGHT

This insidious desire binds us to ego and pride, blinding us to the wisdom that comes from humility. It erects barriers between ourselves and others, stifling growth and breeding conflict. Let go of the compulsion to always be right. Embrace the liberating power of openness, the grace in admitting when you're wrong, and the growth that comes from truly listening.

THE NEED TO BE IN CONTROL

Control is an illusion—a false sense of security that suffocates spontaneity and stifles the divine flow of life. Our desperate attempts to manage every outcome only lead to frustration and anxiety. Surrender this need. Trust in the process, in the divine orchestration of your journey. Allow life to unfold with all its mysteries and surprises, knowing that relinquishing control opens the door to possibilities beyond your imagination.

THE NEED TO LOOK GOOD

When appearances take precedence over authenticity, we betray the expression of our true selves. The masks we wear may shield us from judgment, but they also prevent us from being truly seen and known. Strip away these facades. Stand confidently in your authenticity, for it is in your realness that your true power lies. The world doesn't need another imitation; it needs the unique, unrepeatable expression of *you*.

THE NEED TO BE COMFORTABLE

Comfort zones are cozy but confining. They lull us into complacency and rob us of the exhilaration that comes from stretching beyond perceived limits. True growth demands that we step into the unknown, face our fears, and embrace discomfort. It's through these challenges that we discover resilience, unlock new potentials, and experience the fullness of life.

STEPPING INTO YOUR DESTINY

Now is the time to confront these enemies head-on. By releasing the need to be right, to control, to look good, and to remain comfortable, you liberate yourself to pursue your true purpose with unwavering courage. The world is waiting for what only you can offer—the unique blend of gifts, experiences, and passions that make up your authentic self.

Remember, transformation is not a solitary endeavor. It's a journey walked alongside those who share your vision and values. Stand with your people—those who uplift you, challenge you, and celebrate the unfolding of your true self. Together, you can leave an indelible mark on the world.

A CALL TO ACTION

So I challenge you: Dare to step beyond the familiar confines of your old self. Embrace the uncertainties, the risks, and the adventures that lie ahead. Allow love and courage to propel you forward. Let go of what no longer serves you and make room for the extraordinary. Your life is a testament to the possibility of change, the power of purpose, and the beauty of authenticity. Let your story be a catalyst for others. Let your actions echo into eternity, leaving a legacy of love, hope, and transformation.

THE JOURNEY CONTINUES

As you close this book, know that this is not the end but a glorious beginning. Every day is an opportunity to choose freedom over fear, purpose over complacency, and authenticity over illusion. Embrace the ongoing process of becoming, and never underestimate the impact of a life lived fully awake.

Welcome to your transformation. Welcome to a new way of living, a new way of being. It's time to wake up. It's time to live fully. It's time to become who you were always meant to be. Live with the level of freedom and purpose you were created to experience every single day in this twilight zone of our Upside-Down World we live in.

The world needs your light. It's time to shine.

The best is yet to come.

BIBLIOGRAPHY

Chapter 1
Shattered Illusions
Breaking the Chains of the Past

- Augustine, Saint. *Confessions*. Translated by Henry Chadwick. Oxford: Oxford University Press, 1991.
- Camus, Albert. *The Rebel: An Essay on Man in Revolt*. Translated by Anthony Bower. New York: Vintage Books, 1991.
- Emerson, Ralph Waldo. *Essays: First Series*. Boston: James Munroe and Company, 1841.
- Freud, Sigmund. *The Interpretation of Dreams*. Translated by A.A. Brill. New York: Macmillan, 1913.
- Grover, Tim S. *Relentless: From Good to Great to Unstoppable*. New York: Scribner, 2013.
- Kilbourne, Jeane. *Can't Buy My Love: How Advertising Changes the Way We Think and Feel*. New York: Simon & Schuster, 1999.
- Lamott, Anne. *Traveling Mercies: Some Thoughts on Faith*. New York: Pantheon Books, 1999.
- Robbins, Tony. *Awaken the Giant Within: How to Take Immediate Control of Your Mental, Emotional, Physical and Financial Destiny!*. New York: Free Press, 1991.
- *The Bible*. New International Version. Colorado Springs: International Bible Society, 1984.

Chapter 2
The Ache of Misalignment
Finding Integrity and Wholeness

- Baldwin, James. *Notes of a Native Son*. Boston: Beacon Press, 1955.
- Bonhoeffer, Dietrich. *Life Together: The Classic Exploration of Christian Community*. New York: Harper & Row, 1954.
- Brown, Brené. *The Gifts of Imperfection: Let Go of Who You Think You're Supposed to Be and Embrace Who You Are*. Center City: Hazelden Publishing, 2010.

- Camus, Albert. *The Rebel: An Essay on Man in Revolt*. New York: Vintage International, 1991.
- Jung, Carl G. *Modern Man in Search of a Soul*. London: Routledge, 1933.
- Lewis, C.S. *Mere Christianity*. New York: HarperCollins, 2001.
- Oliver, Mary. *New and Selected Poems, Volume One*. Boston: Beacon Press, 1992.
- Socrates. Quoted in *Plato's Apology*. Translated by Benjamin Jowett. Oxford: Clarendon Press, 1871.
- Teresa of Ávila, Saint. *The Interior Castle*. Translated by E. Allison Peers. New York: Image Books, 1961.

Chapter 3
The Call to Courage
Facing Fear and Finding Your True Path

- Brown, Brené. *The Gifts of Imperfection: Let Go of Who You Think You're Supposed to Be and Embrace Who You Are*. Center City: Hazelden Publishing, 2010.
- Coelho, Paulo. *The Alchemist*. San Francisco: HarperOne, 1993.
- Emerson, Ralph Waldo. *Self-Reliance and Other Essays*. New York: Dover Publications, 1993.
- Frankl, Viktor E. *Man's Search for Meaning*. Boston: Beacon Press, 1959.
- Jeffers, Susan. *Feel the Fear and Do It Anyway*. New York: Ballantine Books, 1987.
- Rowling, J.K. *Very Good Lives: The Fringe Benefits of Failure and the Importance of Imagination*. London: Sphere, 2015.
- Suu Kyi, Aung San. *Freedom from Fear and Other Writings*. Edited by Michael Aris. New York: Penguin, 1995.
- Tutu, Desmond. *No Future Without Forgiveness*. New York: Doubleday, 1999.

Chapter 4
The Power of Purpose
Fueling a Life of Meaning and Impact

- Bonhoeffer, Dietrich. *The Cost of Discipleship*. New York: Touchstone, 1995.

- Brown, Brené. *The Gifts of Imperfection: Let Go of Who You Think You're Supposed to Be and Embrace Who You Are.* Center City: Hazelden Publishing, 2010.
- Frankl, Viktor E. *Man's Search for Meaning.* Boston: Beacon Press, 1959.
- Lewis, C.S. *Mere Christianity.* New York: HarperCollins, 2001.
- Twain, Mark. *Mark Twain's Notebook.* New York: Harper & Brothers, 1935.

Chapter 5
From Setbacks to Stepping Stones
Building Resilience Through Adversity

- Angelou, Maya. *Letter to My Daughter.* New York: Random House, 2008.
- Brown, Brené. *Dare to Lead: Brave Work. Tough Conversations. Whole Hearts.* New York: Random House, 2018.
- Frankl, Viktor E. *Man's Search for Meaning.* Boston: Beacon Press, 1959.
- Mandela, Nelson. *Long Walk to Freedom: The Autobiography of Nelson Mandela.* New York: Little, Brown, and Company, 1994.
- Rogers, Carl. *On Becoming a Person: A Therapist's View of Psychotherapy.* Boston: Houghton Mifflin Harcourt, 1961.
- van der Kolk, Bessel A. *The Body Keeps the Score: Brain, Mind, and Body in the Healing of Trauma.* New York: Viking, 2014.
- Wrosch, Carsten, and Adam M. Grant. *Resilience: The Science of Mastering Life's Greatest Challenges.* Cambridge: Harvard University Press, 2019.

Chapter 6
From Self to Service
Discovering Fulfillment in Giving

- Alcoholics Anonymous. *The Big Book.* New York: Alcoholics Anonymous World Services, Inc., 1939.
- Bonhoeffer, Dietrich. *The Cost of Discipleship.* New York: Touchstone, 1995.
- Frank, Anne. *The Diary of a Young Girl.* New York: Bantam, 1993.
- Gandhi, Mahatma. *The Words of Gandhi.* Edited by Richard Attenborough. New York: Newmarket Press, 1982.

- Gandhi, Mahatma. *All Men Are Brothers: Autobiographical Reflections*. New York: Continuum, 2005.
- Jesus Christ. Matthew 20:28, *The Holy Bible*, New International Version. Grand Rapids: Zondervan, 1978.
- Mother Teresa. *No Greater Love*. New York: New World Library, 2002.
- Schweitzer, Albert. *Out of My Life and Thought: An Autobiography*. New York: Holt Paperbacks, 1990.

Chapter 7
Living in Harmony
Integrating Body, Soul, and Spirit

- Weil, Andrew. *Spontaneous Healing: How to Discover and Enhance Your Body's Natural Ability to Maintain and Heal Itself*. New York: Ballantine Books, 1995.
- Rohn, Jim. *The Art of Exceptional Living*. New York: Simon & Schuster, 1993.
- Lao Tzu. *Tao Te Ching*. Translated by Stephen Mitchell. New York: Harper & Row, 1988.
- Pope John Paul II. *Theology of the Body: Human Love in the Divine Plan*. Boston: Pauline Books & Media, 1997.
- Rohr, Richard. *The Naked Now: Learning to See as the Mystics See*. New York: Crossroad Publishing, 2009.
- Rohn, Jim. "Take care of your body. It's the only place you have to live." Quotation.

Chapter 8
Rooted in Faith
Building a Life that Stands Strong

- Augustine, Saint. *Confessions*. Translated by Henry Chadwick. Oxford: Oxford University Press, 1998.
- Augustine, Saint. "God loves each of us as if there were only one of us." Quotation.
- Chrysostom, John. *Homilies on the Gospel of Matthew*. Nicene and Post-Nicene Fathers, Vol. 10. Edited by Philip Schaff. Grand Rapids: Eerdmans, 1889.
- John of the Cross. *Dark Night of the Soul*. New York: Image Books, 1959.

- Spurgeon, Charles. *Faith*. Grand Rapids: Christian Classics Ethereal Library, 2005.
- Tozer, A.W. *The Knowledge of the Holy: The Attributes of God*. San Francisco: HarperOne, 1961.
- Chambers, Oswald. *My Utmost for His Highest*. Grand Rapids: Discovery House Publishers, 1935.
- Augustine, Saint. *On Faith and the Creed. Nicene and Post-Nicene Fathers*, Vol. 3. Edited by Philip Schaff. Grand Rapids: Eerdmans, 1887.

Chapter 9
The Strength in Softness
Embracing Vulnerability as Power

- Bonhoeffer, Dietrich. *Life Together*. Translated by John W. Doberstein. New York: Harper & Row, 1954.
- Brown, Brené. *Daring Greatly: How the Courage to Be Vulnerable Transforms the Way We Live, Love, Parent, and Lead*. New York: Gotham Books, 2012.
- Brown, Brené. *The Gifts of Imperfection: Let Go of Who You Think You're Supposed to Be and Embrace Who You Are*. Center City: Hazelden, 2010.
- Nouwen, Henri J.M. *The Wounded Healer: Ministry in Contemporary Society*. New York: Image Books, 1979.
- Angelou, Maya. *I Know Why the Caged Bird Sings*. New York: Random House, 1969.

Chapter 10
The Unfinished Journey
Embracing the Path of Ongoing Transformation

- Dyer, Wayne. *The Power of Intention: Learning to Co-Create Your World Your Way*. New York: Hay House, 2004.
- Grover, Tim S. *Relentless: From Good to Great to Unstoppable*. New York: Scribner, 2013.
- Lewis, C.S. *Mere Christianity*. New York: HarperOne, 2001.
- Maxwell, John C. *The 15 Invaluable Laws of Growth: Live Them and Reach Your Potential*. Nashville: Center Street, 2012.
- Robbins, Tony. *Awaken the Giant Within: How to Take Immediate*

Control of Your Mental, Emotional, Physical and Financial Destiny! New York: Free Press, 1991.
- Rilke, Rainer Maria. *Letters to a Young Poet*. Translated by M.D. Herter Norton. New York: W.W. Norton & Company, 2004.

THANK YOU FOR FINISHING THE JOURNEY!

You've just walked through the heart of this book, and I'm honored by your commitment. As a final gift, I'd love to offer you exclusive bonuses and a no-charge coaching call—no strings attached. Simply scan the QR code to claim your rewards, clarify your next steps, and see if working with me is the right fit for your ongoing transformation.

Scan the QR Code:

I appreciate your interest in my book and value your feedback as it helps me improve future versions of this book. I would appreciate it if you could leave your invaluable review on Amazon.com with your feedback. Thank you!